MznLnx

Missing Links Exam Preps

Exam Prep for

Beginning Algebra

Aufmann, Barker, Lockwood, 6th Edition

The MznLnx Exam Prep is your link from the texbook and lecture to your exams.
The MznLnx Exam Preps are unauthorized and comprehensive reviews of your textbooks.

All material provided by MznLnx and Rico Publications (c) 2010
Textbook publishers and textbook authors do not particpate in or contribute to these reviews.

MznLnx

Rico
Publications

Exam Prep for Beginning Algebra
6th Edition
Aufmann, Barker, Lockwood

Publisher: Raymond Houge
Assistant Editor: Michael Rouger
Text and Cover Designer: Lisa Buckner
Marketing Manager: Sara Swagger
Project Manager, Editorial Production: Jerry Emerson
Art Director: Vernon Lowerui

Product Manager: Dave Mason
Editorial Assitant: Rachel Guzmanji
Pedagogy: Debra Long
Cover Image: Jim Reed/Getty Images
Text and Cover Printer: City Printing, Inc.
Compositor: Media Mix, Inc.

(c) 2010 Rico Publications
ALL RIGHTS RESERVED. No part of this work covered by the copyright may be reproduced or used in any form or by an means--graphic, electronic, or mechanical, including photocopying, recording, taping, Web distribution, information storage, and retrieval systems, or in any other manner--without the written permission of the publisher.

For more information about our products, contact us at:
Dave.Mason@RicoPublications.com

For permission to use material from this text or product, submit a request online to:
Dave.Mason@RicoPublications.com

Printed in the United States
ISBN:

Contents

CHAPTER 1
Real Numbers — 1

CHAPTER 2
Variable Expressions — 12

CHAPTER 3
Solving Equations and inequalities — 22

CHAPTER 4
Solving Equations and Inequalities: Applications — 35

CHAPTER 5
Linear Equations and inequalities — 51

CHAPTER 6
Systems of Linear Equations — 64

CHAPTER 7
Polynomials — 74

CHAPTER 8
Factoring — 85

CHAPTER 9
Rational Expressions — 97

CHAPTER 10
Radical Expressions — 110

CHAPTER 11
Quadratic Equations — 114

ANSWER KEY — 117

TO THE STUDENT

COMPREHENSIVE

The *MznLnx* Exam Prep series is designed to help you pass your exams. Editors at MznLnx review your textbooks and then prepare these practice exams to help you master the textbook material. Unlike study guides, workbooks, and practice tests provided by the texbook publisher and textbook authors, *MznLnx* gives you **all** of the material in each chapter in exam form, not just samples, so you can be sure to nail your exam.

MECHANICAL

The MznLnx Exam Prep series creates exams that will help you learn the subject matter as well as test you on your understanding. Each question is designed to help you master the concept. Just working through the exams, you gain an understanding of the subject--its a simple mechanical process that produces success.

INTEGRATED STUDY GUIDE AND REVIEW

MznLnx is not just a set of exams designed to test you, its also a comprehensive review of the subject content. Each exam question is also a review of the concept, making sure that you will get the answer correct without having to go to other sources of material. You learn as you go! Its the easiest way to pass an exam.

HUMOR

Studying can be tedious and dry. MznLnx's instructional design includes moderate humor within the exam questions on occassion, to break the tedium and revitalize the brain

Chapter 1. Real Numbers

1. The _____ of a ring R is defined to be the smallest positive integer n such that n a = 0, for all a in R.
   a. Thing
   b. Characteristic0
   c. Undefined
   d. Undefined

2. An _____ or member of a set is an object that when collected together make up the set.
   a. Element0
   b. Thing
   c. Undefined
   d. Undefined

3. In mathematics, the _____ , or members of a set or more generally a class are all those objects which when collected together make up the set or class.
   a. Elements0
   b. Thing
   c. Undefined
   d. Undefined

4. In mathematics, a _____ can mean either an element of the set {1, 2, 3, ...} (i.e the positive integers or the counting numbers) or an element of the set {0, 1, 2, 3, ...} (i.e. the non-negative integers).
   a. Thing
   b. Natural number0
   c. Undefined
   d. Undefined

5. The _____, the average in everyday English, which is also called the arithmetic _____ (and is distinguished from the geometric _____ or harmonic _____). The average is also called the sample _____. The expected value of a random variable, which is also called the population _____.
   a. Thing
   b. Mean0
   c. Undefined
   d. Undefined

6. In mathematics, a _____ can mean either an element of the set {1, 2, 3, ...} (i.e the positive integers) or an element of the set {0, 1, 2, 3, ...} (i.e. the non-negative integers).
   a. Whole number0
   b. Concept
   c. Undefined
   d. Undefined

7. _____ is a synonym for information.
   a. Thing
   b. Data0
   c. Undefined
   d. Undefined

8. A _____ is a unit of length, usually used to measure distance, in a number of different systems, including Imperial units, United States customary units and Norwegian/Swedish mil. Its size can vary from system to system, but in each is between 1 and 10 kilometers. In contemporary English contexts _____ refers to either:
   a. Thing
   b. Mile0
   c. Undefined
   d. Undefined

9. Claudius Ptolemaeus, known in English as _____, was a Hellenistic mathematician, geographer, astronomer, and astrologer. The Almagest is widely held to be the first systematic treatise on astronomy in antiquity. Babylonian astronomers had developed arithmetical techniques for calculating astronomical phenomena; Greek astronomers such as Hipparchus had produced geometric models for calculating celestial motions; _____, however, clearly derived his geometrical models from selected astronomical observations by his predecessors spanning more than 800 years.
   a. Person
   b. Ptolemy0
   c. Undefined
   d. Undefined

Chapter 1. Real Numbers

10. Leonardo of Pisa (1170s or 1180s – 1250), also known as Leonardo Pisano, Leonardo Bonacci, Leonardo _____, or, most commonly, simply _____, was an Italian mathematician, considered by some "the most talented mathematician of the Middle Ages."
   a. Fibonacci0
   b. Person
   c. Undefined
   d. Undefined

11. A _____ is a one-dimensional picture in which the integers are shown as specially-marked points evenly spaced on a line.
   a. Thing
   b. Number line0
   c. Undefined
   d. Undefined

12. The _____ are the only integral domain whose positive elements are well-ordered, and in which order is preserved by addition. Like the natural numbers, the _____ form a countably infinite set. The set of all _____ is usually denoted in mathematics by a boldface Z .
   a. Integers0
   b. Thing
   c. Undefined
   d. Undefined

13. _____ are the basic objects of study in graph theory. Informally speaking, a graph is a set of objects called points, nodes, or vertices connected by links called lines or edges.
   a. Thing
   b. Graphs0
   c. Undefined
   d. Undefined

14. In mathematics, an _____ is a statement about the relative size or order of two objects.
   a. Inequality0
   b. Thing
   c. Undefined
   d. Undefined

15. In mathematics, an inequality is a statement about the relative size or order of two objects. For example 14 > 10, or 14 is _____ 10.
   a. Greater than0
   b. Thing
   c. Undefined
   d. Undefined

16. In mathematics, the additive inverse, or _____ of a number n is the number that, when added to n, yields zero. The additive inverse of n is denoted −n. For example, 7 is −7, because 7 + (−7) = 0, and the additive inverse of −0.3 is 0.3, because −0.3 + 0.3 = 0.
   a. Thing
   b. Opposite0
   c. Undefined
   d. Undefined

17. In mathematics, the _____ (or modulus) of a real number is its numerical value without regard to its sign.
   a. Absolute value0
   b. Thing
   c. Undefined
   d. Undefined

18. In mathematics, the _____ of a number n is the number that, when added to n, yields zero. The _____ of n is denoted −n. For example, 7 is −7, because 7 + (−7) = 0, and the _____ of −0.3 is 0.3, because −0.3 + 0.3 = 0.
   a. Thing
   b. Additive inverse0
   c. Undefined
   d. Undefined

Chapter 1. Real Numbers

19. _____ element of an element x with respect to a binary operation * with identity element e is an element y such that x * y = y * x = e. In particular,
   a. Inverse0
   b. Thing
   c. Undefined
   d. Undefined

20. In mathematics, the _____ inverse, or opposite, of a number n is the number that, when added to n, yields zero. The _____ inverse of n is denoted −n.
   a. Thing
   b. Additive0
   c. Undefined
   d. Undefined

21. _____, verti-bar, vertical line, divider line, or pipe is the name of the character .
   a. Thing
   b. Vertical bar0
   c. Undefined
   d. Undefined

22. The _____ (symbol _____) and the millibar (symbol mbar, also mb) are units of pressure.
   a. Bar0
   b. Thing
   c. Undefined
   d. Undefined

23. A _____ is a number that is less than zero.
   a. Negative number0
   b. Thing
   c. Undefined
   d. Undefined

24. A _____ is a symbolic representation denoting a quantity or expression. It often represents an "unknown" quantity that has the potential to change.
   a. Variable0
   b. Thing
   c. Undefined
   d. Undefined

25. In business, particularly accounting, a _____ is the time intervals that the accounts, statement, payments, or other calculations cover.
   a. Period0
   b. Thing
   c. Undefined
   d. Undefined

26. In common philosophical language, a proposition or _____, is the content of an assertion, that is, it is true-or-false and defined by the meaning of a particular piece of language.
   a. Concept
   b. Statement0
   c. Undefined
   d. Undefined

27. _____ are objects, characters, or other concrete representations of ideas, concepts, or other abstractions.
   a. Thing
   b. Symbols0
   c. Undefined
   d. Undefined

28. _____ is a physical property of a system that underlies the common notions of hot and cold; something that is hotter has the greater _____.
   a. Temperature0
   b. Thing
   c. Undefined
   d. Undefined

Chapter 1. Real Numbers

29. The _____ of measurement are a globally standardized and modernized form of the metric system.
    a. Thing
    b. Units0
    c. Undefined
    d. Undefined

30. An _____ is a number which is involved in addition. Numbers being added are considered to be the addends.
    a. Thing
    b. Addend0
    c. Undefined
    d. Undefined

31. A _____ is the result of the addition of a set of numbers. The numbers may be natural numbers, complex numbers, matrices, or still more complicated objects. An infinite _____ is a subtle procedure known as a series.
    a. Sum0
    b. Thing
    c. Undefined
    d. Undefined

32. In mathematics, a _____ is the result of multiplying, or an expression that identifies factors to be multiplied.
    a. Thing
    b. Product0
    c. Undefined
    d. Undefined

33. In mathematics, _____ is an elementary arithmetic operation. When one of the numbers is a whole number, _____ is the repeated sum of the other number.
    a. Thing
    b. Multiplication0
    c. Undefined
    d. Undefined

34. In mathematics, factorization (British English: factorisation) or factoring is the decomposition of an object (for example, a number, a polynomial, or a matrix) into a product of other objects, or _____, which when multiplied together give the original.
    a. Thing
    b. Factors0
    c. Undefined
    d. Undefined

35. In mathematics, a _____ is an ordered list of objects. Like a set, it contains members, also called elements or terms, and the number of terms is called the length of the _____. Unlike a set, order matters, and the exact same elements can appear multiple times at different positions in the _____.
    a. Thing
    b. Sequence0
    c. Undefined
    d. Undefined

36. In mathematics, a _____ is the end result of a division problem. It can also be expressed as the number of times the divisor divides into the dividend.
    a. Quotient0
    b. Thing
    c. Undefined
    d. Undefined

37. In mathematics, an _____, mean, or central tendency of a data set refers to a measure of the "middle" or "expected" value of the data set.
    a. Average0
    b. Concept
    c. Undefined
    d. Undefined

38. In mathematics, _____ are essentially word problems that are designed to use mathematical critical thinking in everyday situations.

a. Application problems0
b. Thing
c. Undefined
d. Undefined

39. Acid _____ ratio measures the ability of a company to use its near cash or quick assets to immediately extinguish its current liabilities.
   a. Thing
   b. Test0
   c. Undefined
   d. Undefined

40. _____ or arithmetics is the oldest and most elementary branch of mathematics, used by almost everyone, for tasks ranging from simple daily counting to advanced science and business calculations.
   a. Thing
   b. Arithmetic0
   c. Undefined
   d. Undefined

41. _____ of a list of numbers is the sum of all the members of the list divided by the number of items in the list.
   a. Thing
   b. Arithmetic mean0
   c. Undefined
   d. Undefined

42. _____ is, or relates to, the _____ temperature scale .
   a. Thing
   b. Celsius0
   c. Undefined
   d. Undefined

43. In mathematics, there are several meanings of _____ depending on the subject.
   a. Degree0
   b. Thing
   c. Undefined
   d. Undefined

44. The plus and _____ signs are mathematical symbols used to represent the notions of positive and negative as well as the operations of addition and subtraction.
   a. Minus0
   b. Thing
   c. Undefined
   d. Undefined

45. The _____ of a geographic location is its height above a fixed reference point, often the mean sea level.
   a. Elevation0
   b. Thing
   c. Undefined
   d. Undefined

46. In mathematics, a _____ or rhodonea curve is a sinusoid plotted in polar coordinates.
   a. Thing
   b. Rose0
   c. Undefined
   d. Undefined

47. _____ are a measure of time.
   a. Thing
   b. Minutes0
   c. Undefined
   d. Undefined

48. A _____ of a number is the product of that number with any integer.
   a. Multiple0
   b. Thing
   c. Undefined
   d. Undefined

49. In mathematics, a _____ may be described informally as a number that can be given by an infinite decimal representation.
   a. Real number0
   b. Thing
   c. Undefined
   d. Undefined

50. In mathematics, a _____ number is a number which can be expressed as a ratio of two integers. Non-integer _____ numbers (commonly called fractions) are usually written as the vulgar fraction a / b, where b is not zero.
   a. Rational0
   b. Thing
   c. Undefined
   d. Undefined

51. _____ is the fee paid on borrowed money.
   a. Interest0
   b. Thing
   c. Undefined
   d. Undefined

52. _____ is a set, with some particular properties and usually some additional structure, such as the operations of addition or multiplication, for instance.
   a. Space0
   b. Thing
   c. Undefined
   d. Undefined

53. A _____ is a numeral used to indicate a count. The most common use of the word today is to name the part of a fraction that tells the number or count of equal parts.
   a. Thing
   b. Numerator0
   c. Undefined
   d. Undefined

54. In astronomy, geography, geometry and related sciences and contexts, a plane is said to be _____ at a given point if it is locally perpendicular to the gradient of the gravity field, i.e., with the direction of the gravitational force at that point.
   a. Horizontal0
   b. Thing
   c. Undefined
   d. Undefined

55. A _____ is the part of a fraction that tells how many equal parts make up a whole, and which is used in the name of the fraction: "halves", "thirds", "fourths" or "quarters", "fifths" and so on.
   a. Denominator0
   b. Concept
   c. Undefined
   d. Undefined

56. Mathematical _____ is used to represent ideas.
   a. Thing
   b. Notation0
   c. Undefined
   d. Undefined

57. _____ is the writing of numbers in the base-ten numeral system, which uses various symbols called digits for ten distinct values 0, 1, 2, 3, 4, 5, 6, 7, 8 and 9 to represent numbers
   a. Decimal notation0
   b. Thing
   c. Undefined
   d. Undefined

58. A _____ is the part of the dividend that is left over when the dividend is not evenly divisible by the divisor.

Chapter 1. Real Numbers

a. Remainder0   b. Thing
c. Undefined   d. Undefined

59. A _____ decimal is a decimal fraction which ends after a definite number of digits.
   a. Thing
   b. Terminating0
   c. Undefined
   d. Undefined

60. A _____ decimal is a number whose decimal representation eventually becomes periodic (i.e. the same number sequence _____ indefinitely).
   a. Thing
   b. Repeating0
   c. Undefined
   d. Undefined

61. In mathematics, an _____ number is any real number that is not a rational number- that is, it is a number which cannot be expressed as a fraction m/n, where m and n are integers.
   a. Thing
   b. Irrational0
   c. Undefined
   d. Undefined

62. In mathematics, an _____ is any real number that is not a rational number ¡ª that is, it is a number which cannot be expressed as m/n, where m and n are integers.
   a. Irrational number0
   b. Thing
   c. Undefined
   d. Undefined

63. In mathematics, _____ are any real number that is not a rational number ¡ª that is, it is a number which cannot be expressed as m/n, where m and n are integers.
   a. Irrational numbers0
   b. Thing
   c. Undefined
   d. Undefined

64. Equivalence is the condition of being _____ or essentially equal.
   a. Equivalent0
   b. Thing
   c. Undefined
   d. Undefined

65. The _____ of two integers is the smallest positive integer that is a multiple of both intergers.
   a. Least common multiple0
   b. Thing
   c. Undefined
   d. Undefined

66. In mathematics, the _____ divisor of two non-zero integers, is the largest positive integer that divides both numbers without remainder.
   a. Greatest common0
   b. Thing
   c. Undefined
   d. Undefined

67. In Math the greates common divisor sometimes known as the _____ of two non- zero integers.
   a. Greatest common factor0
   b. Thing
   c. Undefined
   d. Undefined

68. _____ is the largest positive integer that divides both numbers without remainder.

a. Thing
c. Undefined
b. Common Factor0
d. Undefined

69. In mathematics, _____ is the decomposition of an object into a product of other objects, or factors, which when multiplied together give the original.
    a. Thing
    b. Factoring0
    c. Undefined
    d. Undefined

70. The decimal separator is a symbol used to mark the boundary between the integral and the fractional parts of a decimal numeral. Terms implying the symbol used are _____ and decimal comma.
    a. Decimal point0
    b. Concept
    c. Undefined
    d. Undefined

71. In mathematics, the multiplicative inverse of a number x, denoted 1/x or x^{-1}, is the number which, when multiplied by x, yields 1. The multiplicative inverse of x is also called the _____ of x.
    a. Reciprocal0
    b. Thing
    c. Undefined
    d. Undefined

72. In mathematics, a _____ of an integer n, also called a factor of n, is an integer which evenly divides n without leaving a remainder.
    a. Thing
    b. Divisor0
    c. Undefined
    d. Undefined

73. _____ is a payment made by a company to its shareholders
    a. Thing
    b. Dividend0
    c. Undefined
    d. Undefined

74. _____ is a way of expressing a number as a fraction of 100 per cent meaning "per hundred".
    a. Thing
    b. Percent0
    c. Undefined
    d. Undefined

75. A _____ is the sum of a whole number and a proper fraction.
    a. Thing
    b. Mixed number0
    c. Undefined
    d. Undefined

76. In plane geometry, a _____ is a polygon with four equal sides, four right angles, and parallel opposite sides. In algebra, the _____ of a number is that number multiplied by itself.
    a. Thing
    b. Square0
    c. Undefined
    d. Undefined

77. In mathematics, a matrix can be thought of as each row or _____ being a vector. Hence, a space formed by row vectors or _____ vectors are said to be a row space or a _____ space.
    a. Concept
    b. Column0
    c. Undefined
    d. Undefined

Chapter 1. Real Numbers

78. A _____ can refer to a line joining two nonadjacent vertices of a polygon or polyhedron, or in some contexts any upward or downward sloping line. .
  a. Diagonal0
  b. Thing
  c. Undefined
  d. Undefined

79. A _____ is a consumption tax charged at the point of purchase for certain goods and services.
  a. Thing
  b. Sales tax0
  c. Undefined
  d. Undefined

80. A _____ is a special kind of ratio, indicating a relationship between two measurements with different units, such as miles to gallons or cents to pounds.
  a. Rate0
  b. Thing
  c. Undefined
  d. Undefined

81. In finance and economics, _____ is the process of finding the present value of an amount of cash at some future date, and along with compounding cash forms the basis of time value of money calculations.
  a. Thing
  b. Discount0
  c. Undefined
  d. Undefined

82. The _____ is different from a more normal interest rate.
  a. Discount rate0
  b. Thing
  c. Undefined
  d. Undefined

83. In arithmetic and algebra, when a number or expression is both preceded and followed by a binary operation, an _____ is required for which operation should be applied first.
  a. Order of operations0
  b. Thing
  c. Undefined
  d. Undefined

84. _____ is a mathematical operation, written a^n, involving two numbers, the base a and the exponent n.
  a. Thing
  b. Exponentiating0
  c. Undefined
  d. Undefined

85. _____ is a mathematical operation, written a^n, involving two numbers, the base a and the exponent n.
  a. Exponentiation0
  b. Thing
  c. Undefined
  d. Undefined

86. In mathematics, _____ growth occurs when the growth rate of a function is always proportional to the function's current size.
  a. Thing
  b. Exponential0
  c. Undefined
  d. Undefined

87. An _____ is a combination of numbers, operators, grouping symbols and/or free variables and bound variables arranged in a meaningful way which can be evaluated..
  a. Expression0
  b. Thing
  c. Undefined
  d. Undefined

Chapter 1. Real Numbers

88. _____ has many meanings, most of which simply .
    a. Power0
    b. Thing
    c. Undefined
    d. Undefined

89. A _____ is a three-dimensional solid object bounded by six square faces, facets, or sides, with three meeting at each vertex.
    a. Thing
    b. Cube0
    c. Undefined
    d. Undefined

90. _____ is a notation for writing numbers that is often used by scientists and mathematicians to make it easier to write large and small numbers.
    a. Scientific notation0
    b. Thing
    c. Undefined
    d. Undefined

91. _____ was a highly influential French philosopher, mathematician, scientist, and writer. Dubbed the "Founder of Modern Philosophy", and the "Father of Modern Mathematics". His theories provided the basis for the calculus of Newton and Leibniz, by applying infinitesimal calculus to the tangent line problem, thus permitting the evolution of that branch of modern mathematics
    a. Person
    b. Descartes0
    c. Undefined
    d. Undefined

92. _____, either of the curved-bracket punctuation marks that together make a set of _____
    a. Parentheses0
    b. Thing
    c. Undefined
    d. Undefined

93. The traditional _____ are addition, subtraction, multiplication and division, although more advanced operations (such as manipulations of percentages, square root, exponentiation, and logarithmic functions) are also sometimes included in this subject.
    a. Concept
    b. Arithmetic operations0
    c. Undefined
    d. Undefined

94. In abstract algebra, _____ consists of sets with binary operations that satisfy certain axioms.
    a. Grouping0
    b. Thing
    c. Undefined
    d. Undefined

95. The _____ is a thermodynamic (absolute) temperature scale where absolute zero—the coldest possible temperature—is defined as being equivalent to zero kelvin (0 K).
    a. Kelvin scale0
    b. Thing
    c. Undefined
    d. Undefined

96. In Euclidean geometry, a uniform _____ is a linear transformation that enlargers or diminishes objects, and whose _____ factor is the same in all directions. This is also called homothethy.
    a. Scale0
    b. Thing
    c. Undefined
    d. Undefined

Chapter 1. Real Numbers

97. Celsius is, or relates to, the Celsius temperature scale (previously known as the centigrade scale). The degree Celsius (symbol: °C) can refer to a specific temperature on the _____ as well as serve as unit increment to indicate a temperature interval (a difference between two temperatures or an uncertainty).
   a. Celsius Scale0
   b. Concept
   c. Undefined
   d. Undefined

98. The deductive-nomological model is a formalized view of scientific _____ in natural language.
   a. Explanation0
   b. Thing
   c. Undefined
   d. Undefined

99. A _____ occurs when an entity spends more money than it takes in. The opposite is a budget surplus.
   a. Thing
   b. Federal deficit0
   c. Undefined
   d. Undefined

100. In mathematics, defined and _____ are used to explain whether or not expressions have meaningful, sensible, and unambiguous values.
   a. Undefined0
   b. Thing
   c. Undefined
   d. Undefined

101. _____ or investing is a term with several closely-related meanings in business management, finance and economics, related to saving or deferring consumption.
   a. Thing
   b. Investment0
   c. Undefined
   d. Undefined

102. _____ are activities that are governed by a set of rules or customs and often engaged in competitively.
   a. Sports0
   b. Thing
   c. Undefined
   d. Undefined

103. _____ is the transport of people on a trip/journey or the process or time involved in a person or object moving from one location to another.
   a. Thing
   b. Travel0
   c. Undefined
   d. Undefined

104. A _____ is a compensation which workers receive in exchange for their labor.
   a. Wage0
   b. Thing
   c. Undefined
   d. Undefined

Chapter 2. Variable Expressions

1. A _____ is a symbolic representation denoting a quantity or expression. It often represents an "unknown" quantity that has the potential to change.
   a. Variable0
   b. Thing
   c. Undefined
   d. Undefined

2. An _____ is a combination of numbers, operators, grouping symbols and/or free variables and bound variables arranged in a meaningful way which can be evaluated..
   a. Expression0
   b. Thing
   c. Undefined
   d. Undefined

3. _____ is a branch of mathematics concerning the study of structure, relation and quantity.
   a. Algebra0
   b. Concept
   c. Undefined
   d. Undefined

4. In mathematics, the additive inverse, or _____ of a number n is the number that, when added to n, yields zero. The additive inverse of n is denoted −n. For example, 7 is −7, because 7 + (−7) = 0, and the additive inverse of −0.3 is 0.3, because −0.3 + 0.3 = 0.
   a. Opposite0
   b. Thing
   c. Undefined
   d. Undefined

5. In mathematics, the _____ of a number n is the number that, when added to n, yields zero. The _____ of n is denoted −n. For example, 7 is −7, because 7 + (−7) = 0, and the _____ of −0.3 is 0.3, because −0.3 + 0.3 = 0.
   a. Additive inverse0
   b. Thing
   c. Undefined
   d. Undefined

6. An _____ is a number which is involved in addition. Numbers being added are considered to be the addends.
   a. Addend0
   b. Thing
   c. Undefined
   d. Undefined

7. In mathematics and the mathematical sciences, a _____ is a fixed, but possibly unspecified, value. This is in contrast to a variable, which is not fixed.
   a. Constant0
   b. Thing
   c. Undefined
   d. Undefined

8. _____ is a fixed, but possibly unspecified, value. This is in contrast to a variable, which is not fixed.
   a. Constant term0
   b. Thing
   c. Undefined
   d. Undefined

9. _____ is the fee paid on borrowed money.
   a. Thing
   b. Interest0
   c. Undefined
   d. Undefined

10. In mathematics, a _____ is a constant multiplicative factor of a certain object. The object can be such things as a variable, a vector, a function, etc. For example, the _____ of $9x^2$ is 9.
    a. Thing
    b. Coefficient0
    c. Undefined
    d. Undefined

Chapter 2. Variable Expressions

11. _____ is a mathematical operation, written a^n, involving two numbers, the base a and the exponent n.
    a. Exponentiating0
    b. Thing
    c. Undefined
    d. Undefined

12. _____ is a mathematical operation, written a^n, involving two numbers, the base a and the exponent n.
    a. Exponentiation0
    b. Thing
    c. Undefined
    d. Undefined

13. _____, Greek for "knowledge of nature," is the branch of science concerned with the discovery and characterization of universal laws which govern matter, energy, space, and time.
    a. Physics0
    b. Thing
    c. Undefined
    d. Undefined

14. In mathematics, _____ expressions is used to reduce the expression into the lowest possible term.
    a. Simplifying0
    b. Thing
    c. Undefined
    d. Undefined

15. In arithmetic and algebra, when a number or expression is both preceded and followed by a binary operation, an _____ is required for which operation should be applied first.
    a. Thing
    b. Order of operations0
    c. Undefined
    d. Undefined

16. In mathematics, a _____ is a quadric surface, with the following equation in Cartesian coordinates: $(x/_a)^2 + (y/_b)^2 = 1$.
    a. Thing
    b. Cylinder0
    c. Undefined
    d. Undefined

17. In geometry, a _____ (Greek words diairo = divide and metro = measure) of a circle is any straight line segment that passes through the centre and whose endpoints are on the circular boundary, or, in more modern usage, the length of such a line segment. When using the word in the more modern sense, one speaks of the _____ rather than a _____, because all diameters of a circle have the same length. This length is twice the radius. The _____ of a circle is also the longest chord that the circle has.
    a. Thing
    b. Diameter0
    c. Undefined
    d. Undefined

18. The _____ of a solid object is the three-dimensional concept of how much space it occupies, often quantified numerically.
    a. Thing
    b. Volume0
    c. Undefined
    d. Undefined

19. _____ is a three-dimensional geometric shape formed by straight lines through a fixed point vertex to the points of a fixed curve directrix.
    a. Right circular cone0
    b. Thing
    c. Undefined
    d. Undefined

20. A _____ is a three-dimensional geometric shape formed by straight lines through a fixed point (vertex) to the points of a fixed curve (directrix)
   a. Concept
   b. Cone0
   c. Undefined
   d. Undefined

21. In common philosophical language, a proposition or _____, is the content of an assertion, that is, it is true-or-false and defined by the meaning of a particular piece of language.
   a. Statement0
   b. Concept
   c. Undefined
   d. Undefined

22. In classical geometry, a _____ of a circle or sphere is any line segment from its center to its boundary. By extension, the _____ of a circle or sphere is the length of any such segment. The _____ is half the diameter. In science and engineering the term _____ of curvature is commonly used as a synonym for _____.
   a. Radius0
   b. Thing
   c. Undefined
   d. Undefined

23. In mathematics, a _____ is the set of all points in three-dimensional space (R^3) which are at distance r from a fixed point of that space, where r is a positive real number called the radius of the _____. The fixed point is called the center or centre, and is not part of the _____ itself.
   a. Thing
   b. Sphere0
   c. Undefined
   d. Undefined

24. A _____ is a quadrilateral, which is defined as a shape with four sides, which has a pair of parallel sides.
   a. Trapezoid0
   b. Thing
   c. Undefined
   d. Undefined

25. In mathematics, a _____ can mean either an element of the set {1, 2, 3, ...} (i.e the positive integers or the counting numbers) or an element of the set {0, 1, 2, 3, ...} (i.e. the non-negative integers).
   a. Natural number0
   b. Thing
   c. Undefined
   d. Undefined

26. In mathematics, an inequality is a statement about the relative size or order of two objects. For example 14 > 10, or 14 is _____ 10.
   a. Thing
   b. Greater than0
   c. Undefined
   d. Undefined

27. In mathematics, a _____ is a mathematical statement which appears likely to be true, but has not been formally proven to be true under the rules of mathematical logic.
   a. Conjecture0
   b. Concept
   c. Undefined
   d. Undefined

28. In mathematics, a _____ may be described informally as a number that can be given by an infinite decimal representation.
   a. Real number0
   b. Thing
   c. Undefined
   d. Undefined

Chapter 2. Variable Expressions

29. The _____ is a property of multiplication or addition where the product or sum remains the same, regardless of whether or not the order of the addends or factors are changed.
    a. Thing
    b. Commutative property0
    c. Undefined
    d. Undefined

30. A _____ is the result of the addition of a set of numbers. The numbers may be natural numbers, complex numbers, matrices, or still more complicated objects. An infinite _____ is a subtle procedure known as a series.
    a. Sum0
    b. Thing
    c. Undefined
    d. Undefined

31. In mathematics, _____ is an elementary arithmetic operation. When one of the numbers is a whole number, _____ is the repeated sum of the other number.
    a. Thing
    b. Multiplication0
    c. Undefined
    d. Undefined

32. In mathematics, a _____ is the result of multiplying, or an expression that identifies factors to be multiplied.
    a. Thing
    b. Product0
    c. Undefined
    d. Undefined

33. In mathematics, factorization (British English: factorisation) or factoring is the decomposition of an object (for example, a number, a polynomial, or a matrix) into a product of other objects, or _____, which when multiplied together give the original.
    a. Factors0
    b. Thing
    c. Undefined
    d. Undefined

34. In mathematics, _____ is a property that a binary operation can have. Within an expression containing two or more of the same associative operators in a row, the order of operations does not matter as long as the sequence of the operands is not changed.
    a. Thing
    b. Associativity0
    c. Undefined
    d. Undefined

35. _____, either of the curved-bracket punctuation marks that together make a set of _____
    a. Thing
    b. Parentheses0
    c. Undefined
    d. Undefined

36. _____ element of an element x with respect to a binary operation * with identity element e is an element y such that x * y = y * x = e. In particular,
    a. Thing
    b. Inverse0
    c. Undefined
    d. Undefined

37. In mathematics, the _____ inverse, or opposite, of a number n is the number that, when added to n, yields zero. The _____ inverse of n is denoted −n.
    a. Additive0
    b. Thing
    c. Undefined
    d. Undefined

Chapter 2. Variable Expressions

38. In mathematics, the multiplicative inverse of a number x, denoted 1/x or x^{-1}, is the number which, when multiplied by x, yields 1. The multiplicative inverse of x is also called the _____ of x.
    a. Reciprocal0
    b. Thing
    c. Undefined
    d. Undefined

39. In mathematics, and in particular in abstract algebra, the _____ is a property of binary operations that generalises the distributive law from elementary algebra.
    a. Distributive property0
    b. Thing
    c. Undefined
    d. Undefined

40. In abstract algebra, _____ consists of sets with binary operations that satisfy certain axioms.
    a. Grouping0
    b. Thing
    c. Undefined
    d. Undefined

41. _____ are objects, characters, or other concrete representations of ideas, concepts, or other abstractions.
    a. Thing
    b. Symbols0
    c. Undefined
    d. Undefined

42. In mathematics, the _____ inverse of a number x, denoted 1/x or x^{-1}, is the number which, when multiplied by x, yields 1. The _____ inverse of x is also called the reciprocal of x.
    a. Multiplicative0
    b. Thing
    c. Undefined
    d. Undefined

43. _____ has many meanings, most of which simply .
    a. Power0
    b. Thing
    c. Undefined
    d. Undefined

44. The plus and _____ signs are mathematical symbols used to represent the notions of positive and negative as well as the operations of addition and subtraction.
    a. Minus0
    b. Thing
    c. Undefined
    d. Undefined

45. A _____ is a three-dimensional solid object bounded by six square faces, facets, or sides, with three meeting at each vertex.
    a. Thing
    b. Cube0
    c. Undefined
    d. Undefined

46. In mathematics, a _____ is the end result of a division problem. It can also be expressed as the number of times the divisor divides into the dividend.
    a. Thing
    b. Quotient0
    c. Undefined
    d. Undefined

47. A _____ is a quantity that denotes the proportional amount or magnitude of one quantity relative to another.
    a. Ratio0
    b. Thing
    c. Undefined
    d. Undefined

Chapter 2. Variable Expressions 17

48. In plane geometry, a _____ is a polygon with four equal sides, four right angles, and parallel opposite sides. In algebra, the _____ of a number is that number multiplied by itself.
  a. Square0
  b. Thing
  c. Undefined
  d. Undefined

49. _____ is a synonym for information.
  a. Data0
  b. Thing
  c. Undefined
  d. Undefined

50. _____ is a kind of property which exists as magnitude or multitude. It is among the basic classes of things along with quality, substance, change, and relation.
  a. Amount0
  b. Thing
  c. Undefined
  d. Undefined

51. A _____ is a form of collective investment that pools money from many investors and invests their money in stocks, bonds, short-term money market instruments, and/or other securities.
  a. Thing
  b. Mutual fund0
  c. Undefined
  d. Undefined

52. Equivalence is the condition of being _____ or essentially equal.
  a. Thing
  b. Equivalent0
  c. Undefined
  d. Undefined

53. In mathematical logic, a Gödel numbering (or Gödel _____) is a function that assigns to each symbol and well-formed formula of some formal language a unique natural number called its Gödel number.
  a. Code0
  b. Thing
  c. Undefined
  d. Undefined

54. _____ are activities that are governed by a set of rules or customs and often engaged in competitively.
  a. Sports0
  b. Thing
  c. Undefined
  d. Undefined

55. _____ is a form of periodic payment from an employer to an employee, which is specified in an employment contract.
  a. Gross pay0
  b. Thing
  c. Undefined
  d. Undefined

56. A _____ is a form of periodic payment from an employer to an employee, which is specified in an employment contract.
  a. Thing
  b. Salary0
  c. Undefined
  d. Undefined

57. A _____, as defined by the International Astronomical Union, is a celestial body orbiting a star or stellar remnant that is massive enough to be rounded by its own gravity, not massive enough to cause thermonuclear fusion in its core, and has cleared its neighboring region of planetesimals.

18   *Chapter 2. Variable Expressions*

a. Planet0   b. Thing
c. Undefined   d. Undefined

58. _____ is a state located in the southern and southwestern regions of the United States of America.
    a. Thing   b. Texas0
    c. Undefined   d. Undefined

59. In geometry, a _____ is defined as a quadrilateral where all four of its angles are right angles.
    a. Thing   b. Rectangle0
    c. Undefined   d. Undefined

60. _____ is a mathematical science pertaining to the collection, analysis, interpretation or explanation, and presentation of data. It is applicable to a wide variety of academic disciplines, from the physical and social sciences to the humanities.
    a. Thing   b. Statistics0
    c. Undefined   d. Undefined

61. The _____ is the total number of human beings alive on the planet Earth at a given time.
    a. Thing   b. World population0
    c. Undefined   d. Undefined

62. The population _____ is the total number of human beings alive on the planet Earth at a given time.
    a. Of the world0   b. Thing
    c. Undefined   d. Undefined

63. _____ is a business term for the amount of money that a company receives from its activities in a given period, mostly from sales of products and/or services to customers
    a. Thing   b. Revenue0
    c. Undefined   d. Undefined

64. In sociology and biology a _____ is the collection of people or organisms of a particular species living in a given geographic area or space, usually measured by a census.
    a. Population0   b. Thing
    c. Undefined   d. Undefined

65. The _____ is the United States federal government agency that collects taxes and enforces the internal revenue laws.
    a. Thing   b. Internal Revenue Service0
    c. Undefined   d. Undefined

66. _____ is a payment made by a company to its shareholders
    a. Dividend0   b. Thing
    c. Undefined   d. Undefined

67. A _____ is one of the basic shapes of geometry: a polygon with three vertices and three sides which are straight line segments.

Chapter 2. Variable Expressions

    a. Triangle0
    b. Thing
    c. Undefined
    d. Undefined

68. A _____ is a function that assigns a number to subsets of a given set.
    a. Thing
    b. Measure0
    c. Undefined
    d. Undefined

69. In mathematics, there are several meanings of _____ depending on the subject.
    a. Thing
    b. Degree0
    c. Undefined
    d. Undefined

70. _____ is the transport of people on a trip/journey or the process or time involved in a person or object moving from one location to another.
    a. Travel0
    b. Thing
    c. Undefined
    d. Undefined

71. A _____ is a special kind of ratio, indicating a relationship between two measurements with different units, such as miles to gallons or cents to pounds.
    a. Rate0
    b. Thing
    c. Undefined
    d. Undefined

72. A _____ is a compensation which workers receive in exchange for their labor.
    a. Wage0
    b. Thing
    c. Undefined
    d. Undefined

73. _____ is the amount of time someone works beyond normal working hours.
    a. Compensatory time0
    b. Thing
    c. Undefined
    d. Undefined

74. The process of sending accounts to customers for goods or services is called _____.
    a. Billing0
    b. Thing
    c. Undefined
    d. Undefined

75. _____ are a measure of time.
    a. Minutes0
    b. Thing
    c. Undefined
    d. Undefined

76. The _____, the average in everyday English, which is also called the arithmetic _____ (and is distinguished from the geometric _____ or harmonic _____). The average is also called the sample _____. The expected value of a random variable, which is also called the population _____.
    a. Thing
    b. Mean0
    c. Undefined
    d. Undefined

77. A frame of _____ is a particular perspective from which the universe is observed.

Chapter 2. Variable Expressions

a. Reference0
b. Thing
c. Undefined
d. Undefined

78. In mathematics, the word _____ is used informally to refer to certain distinct bodies of knowledge about mathematics.
a. Theoretical0
b. Thing
c. Undefined
d. Undefined

79. A _____ is a unit of length, usually used to measure distance, in a number of different systems, including Imperial units, United States customary units and Norwegian/Swedish mil. Its size can vary from system to system, but in each is between 1 and 10 kilometers. In contemporary English contexts _____ refers to either:
a. Mile0
b. Thing
c. Undefined
d. Undefined

80. The _____ are the only integral domain whose positive elements are well-ordered, and in which order is preserved by addition. Like the natural numbers, the _____ form a countably infinite set. The set of all _____ is usually denoted in mathematics by a boldface Z .
a. Integers0
b. Thing
c. Undefined
d. Undefined

81. In mathematics, a _____ of an integer n, also called a factor of n, is an integer which evenly divides n without leaving a remainder.
a. Divisor0
b. Thing
c. Undefined
d. Undefined

82. In Euclidean geometry, a _____ is the set of all points in a plane at a fixed distance, called the radius, from a given point, the center.
a. Thing
b. Circle0
c. Undefined
d. Undefined

83. A _____ (so called because it can be arranged into a triangle) is the sum of the n natural numbers from 1 to n.
a. Triangular number0
b. Thing
c. Undefined
d. Undefined

84. A _____ is a negotiable instrument instructing a financial institution to pay a specific amount of a specific currency from a specific demand account held in the maker/depositor's name with that institution. Both the maker and payee may be natural persons or legal entities.
a. Thing
b. Check0
c. Undefined
d. Undefined

85. The _____ is that number multiplied by itself.
a. Thing
b. Square of a number0
c. Undefined
d. Undefined

86. Compass and straightedge or ruler-and-compass _____ is the _____ of lengths or angles using only an idealized ruler and compass.

Chapter 2. Variable Expressions

    a. Thing
    c. Undefined
    b. Construction0
    d. Undefined

87. _____ is a term used in accounting, economics and finance with reference to the fact that assets with finite lives lose value over time.
    a. Depreciation0
    b. Thing
    c. Undefined
    d. Undefined

88. _____ is the level of functional and/or metabolic efficiency of an organism at both the micro level.
    a. Thing
    b. Health0
    c. Undefined
    d. Undefined

89. _____ or investing is a term with several closely-related meanings in business management, finance and economics, related to saving or deferring consumption.
    a. Investment0
    b. Thing
    c. Undefined
    d. Undefined

90. In chemistry, a _____ is substance made by combining two or more different materials in such a way that no chemical reaction occurs.
    a. Mixture0
    b. Thing
    c. Undefined
    d. Undefined

91. A _____ is a method of using property as security for the payment of a debt.
    a. Thing
    b. Mortgage0
    c. Undefined
    d. Undefined

92. _____ is a set, with some particular properties and usually some additional structure, such as the operations of addition or multiplication, for instance.
    a. Thing
    b. Space0
    c. Undefined
    d. Undefined

93. In mathematics, a _____ is any one of several different types of functions, mappings, operations, or transformations.
    a. Projection0
    b. Thing
    c. Undefined
    d. Undefined

94. _____ forms part of thinking. Considered the most complex of all intellectual functions, _____ has been defined as higher-order cognitive process that requires the modulation and control of more routine or fundamental skills.
    a. Thing
    b. Problem solving0
    c. Undefined
    d. Undefined

Chapter 3. Solving Equations and inequalities

1. Two mathematical objects are equal if and only if they are precisely the same in every way. This defines a binary relation, _____, denoted by the sign of _____ "=" in such a way that the statement "x = y" means that x and y are equal.
   a. Thing
   b. Equality0
   c. Undefined
   d. Undefined

2. An _____ is a combination of numbers, operators, grouping symbols and/or free variables and bound variables arranged in a meaningful way which can be evaluated..
   a. Expression0
   b. Thing
   c. Undefined
   d. Undefined

3. _____ is the fee paid on borrowed money.
   a. Thing
   b. Interest0
   c. Undefined
   d. Undefined

4. _____ (March 14, 1879 - April 18, 1955) was a German-born theoretical physicist who is best known for his theory of relativity and specifically mass-energy equivalence, $E = mc^2$.
   a. Person
   b. Albert Einstein0
   c. Undefined
   d. Undefined

5. A _____ is a symbolic representation denoting a quantity or expression. It often represents an "unknown" quantity that has the potential to change.
   a. Variable0
   b. Thing
   c. Undefined
   d. Undefined

6. In arithmetic and algebra, when a number or expression is both preceded and followed by a binary operation, an _____ is required for which operation should be applied first.
   a. Thing
   b. Order of operations0
   c. Undefined
   d. Undefined

7. The _____, the average in everyday English, which is also called the arithmetic _____ (and is distinguished from the geometric _____ or harmonic _____). The average is also called the sample _____. The expected value of a random variable, which is also called the population _____.
   a. Thing
   b. Mean0
   c. Undefined
   d. Undefined

8. In mathematics and the mathematical sciences, a _____ is a fixed, but possibly unspecified, value. This is in contrast to a variable, which is not fixed.
   a. Constant0
   b. Thing
   c. Undefined
   d. Undefined

9. In banking and accountancy, the outstanding _____ is the amount of money owned, or due, that remains in a deposit account or a loan account at a given date, after all past remittances, payments and withdrawal have been accounted for.
   a. Balance0
   b. Thing
   c. Undefined
   d. Undefined

Chapter 3. Solving Equations and inequalities

10. In mathematics, the additive inverse, or _____ of a number n is the number that, when added to n, yields zero. The additive inverse of n is denoted −n. For example, 7 is −7, because 7 + (−7) = 0, and the additive inverse of −0.3 is 0.3, because −0.3 + 0.3 = 0.
    a. Opposite0
    b. Thing
    c. Undefined
    d. Undefined

11. In mathematics, the _____ of a number n is the number that, when added to n, yields zero. The _____ of n is denoted −n. For example, 7 is −7, because 7 + (−7) = 0, and the _____ of −0.3 is 0.3, because −0.3 + 0.3 = 0.
    a. Additive inverse0
    b. Thing
    c. Undefined
    d. Undefined

12. A _____ is a negotiable instrument instructing a financial institution to pay a specific amount of a specific currency from a specific demand account held in the maker/depositor's name with that institution. Both the maker and payee may be natural persons or legal entities.
    a. Thing
    b. Check0
    c. Undefined
    d. Undefined

13. _____ is a fixed, but possibly unspecified, value. This is in contrast to a variable, which is not fixed.
    a. Thing
    b. Constant term0
    c. Undefined
    d. Undefined

14. In mathematics, _____ is an elementary arithmetic operation. When one of the numbers is a whole number, _____ is the repeated sum of the other number.
    a. Thing
    b. Multiplication0
    c. Undefined
    d. Undefined

15. In mathematics, the multiplicative inverse of a number x, denoted $1/x$ or x^{-1}, is the number which, when multiplied by x, yields 1. The multiplicative inverse of x is also called the _____ of x.
    a. Thing
    b. Reciprocal0
    c. Undefined
    d. Undefined

16. In mathematics, a _____ is a constant multiplicative factor of a certain object. The object can be such things as a variable, a vector, a function, etc. For example, the _____ of $9x^2$ is 9.
    a. Coefficient0
    b. Thing
    c. Undefined
    d. Undefined

17. Equivalence is the condition of being _____ or essentially equal.
    a. Equivalent0
    b. Thing
    c. Undefined
    d. Undefined

18. _____ is the transport of people on a trip/journey or the process or time involved in a person or object moving from one location to another.
    a. Travel0
    b. Thing
    c. Undefined
    d. Undefined

Chapter 3. Solving Equations and inequalities

19. In mathematics, _____ are essentially word problems that are designed to use mathematical critical thinking in everyday situations.
    a. Thing
    b. Application problems0
    c. Undefined
    d. Undefined

20. In Euclidean geometry, a _____ is the set of all points in a plane at a fixed distance, called the radius, from a given point, the center.
    a. Thing
    b. Circle0
    c. Undefined
    d. Undefined

21. A _____ is a special kind of ratio, indicating a relationship between two measurements with different units, such as miles to gallons or cents to pounds.
    a. Rate0
    b. Thing
    c. Undefined
    d. Undefined

22. A _____ is a unit of length, usually used to measure distance, in a number of different systems, including Imperial units, United States customary units and Norwegian/Swedish mil. Its size can vary from system to system, but in each is between 1 and 10 kilometers. In contemporary English contexts _____ refers to either:
    a. Mile0
    b. Thing
    c. Undefined
    d. Undefined

23. _____ is a unit of speed, expressing the number of international miles covered per hour.
    a. Thing
    b. Miles per hour0
    c. Undefined
    d. Undefined

24. _____ are a measure of time.
    a. Minutes0
    b. Thing
    c. Undefined
    d. Undefined

25. A _____ is the result of the addition of a set of numbers. The numbers may be natural numbers, complex numbers, matrices, or still more complicated objects. An infinite _____ is a subtle procedure known as a series.
    a. Thing
    b. Sum0
    c. Undefined
    d. Undefined

26. In mathematics, a _____ is a two-dimensional manifold or surface that is perfectly flat.
    a. Plane0
    b. Thing
    c. Undefined
    d. Undefined

27. In mathematics, _____ are two-dimensional manifolds or surfaces that are perfectly flat.
    a. Planes0
    b. Thing
    c. Undefined
    d. Undefined

28. _____ is a way of expressing a number as a fraction of 100 per cent meaning "per hundred".
    a. Thing
    b. Percent0
    c. Undefined
    d. Undefined

Chapter 3. Solving Equations and inequalities

29. _____ is a kind of property which exists as magnitude or multitude. It is among the basic classes of things along with quality, substance, change, and relation.
    a. Amount0
    b. Thing
    c. Undefined
    d. Undefined

30. In geometry, the _____ of an object is a point in some sense in the middle of the object.
    a. Thing
    b. Center0
    c. Undefined
    d. Undefined

31. In sociology and biology a _____ is the collection of people or organisms of a particular species living in a given geographic area or space, usually measured by a census.
    a. Population0
    b. Thing
    c. Undefined
    d. Undefined

32. An _____ is the fee paid on borrow money.
    a. Interest rate0
    b. Concept
    c. Undefined
    d. Undefined

33. _____ or investing is a term with several closely-related meanings in business management, finance and economics, related to saving or deferring consumption.
    a. Thing
    b. Investment0
    c. Undefined
    d. Undefined

34. A _____ is a system of payment named after the small plastic card issued to users of the system.
    a. Thing
    b. Credit card0
    c. Undefined
    d. Undefined

35. _____ finance, in finance, a debt security, issued by Issuer
    a. Bond0
    b. Thing
    c. Undefined
    d. Undefined

36. In business, particularly accounting, a _____ is the time intervals that the accounts, statement, payments, or other calculations cover.
    a. Thing
    b. Period0
    c. Undefined
    d. Undefined

37. In chemistry, a _____ is substance made by combining two or more different materials in such a way that no chemical reaction occurs.
    a. Thing
    b. Mixture0
    c. Undefined
    d. Undefined

38. U.S. liquid _____ is legally defined as 231 cubic inches, and is equal to 3.785411784 litres or abotu 0.13368 cubic feet. This is the most common definition of a _____. The U.S. fluid ounce is defined as 1/128 of a U.S. _____.

Chapter 3. Solving Equations and inequalities

a. Thing
b. Gallon0
c. Undefined
d. Undefined

39. In mathematics, an inequality is a statement about the relative size or order of two objects. For example 14 > 10, or 14 is _____ 10.
a. Thing
b. Greater than0
c. Undefined
d. Undefined

40. _____ is the level of functional and/or metabolic efficiency of an organism at both the micro level.
a. Thing
b. Health0
c. Undefined
d. Undefined

41. A _____ is a unit of length in the metric system, equal to one thousand metres, the current SI base unit of length
a. Thing
b. Kilometer0
c. Undefined
d. Undefined

42. In mathematics, an _____, mean, or central tendency of a data set refers to a measure of the "middle" or "expected" value of the data set.
a. Concept
b. Average0
c. Undefined
d. Undefined

43. In botany, _____ are above-ground plant organs specialized for photosynthesis. Their characteristics are typically analyzed by using Fiobonacci's sequences.
a. Thing
b. Leaves0
c. Undefined
d. Undefined

44. _____ is a form of periodic payment from an employer to an employee, which is specified in an employment contract.
a. Gross pay0
b. Thing
c. Undefined
d. Undefined

45. A _____ is a form of periodic payment from an employer to an employee, which is specified in an employment contract.
a. Salary0
b. Thing
c. Undefined
d. Undefined

46. _____ is the ability to hold, receive or absorb, or a measure thereof, similar to the concept of volume.
a. Capacity0
b. Concept
c. Undefined
d. Undefined

47. In mathematics, a _____ can mean either an element of the set {1, 2, 3, ...} (i.e the positive integers) or an element of the set {0, 1, 2, 3, ...} (i.e. the non-negative integers).
a. Concept
b. Whole number0
c. Undefined
d. Undefined

48. _____ is a synonym for information.

Chapter 3. Solving Equations and inequalities 27

   a. Data0
   b. Thing
   c. Undefined
   d. Undefined

49. The population _____ is the total number of human beings alive on the planet Earth at a given time.
   a. Of the world0
   b. Thing
   c. Undefined
   d. Undefined

50. In mathematics, a _____ is the result of multiplying, or an expression that identifies factors to be multiplied.
   a. Product0
   b. Thing
   c. Undefined
   d. Undefined

51. A _____ is an individual or household that purchases and uses goods and services generated within the economy.
   a. Consumer0
   b. Thing
   c. Undefined
   d. Undefined

52. _____ usually refers to money in the form of liquid currency, such as banknotes or coins.
   a. Thing
   b. Cash0
   c. Undefined
   d. Undefined

53. In mathematics, _____ refers to the rewriting of an expression into a simpler form.
   a. Thing
   b. Reduction0
   c. Undefined
   d. Undefined

54. Multiple Signal Classification, also known as _____, is an algorithm used for frequency estimation and emitter location.
   a. Music0
   b. Thing
   c. Undefined
   d. Undefined

55. In mathematics, a subset of Euclidean space R^n is called _____ if it is closed and bounded.
   a. Compact0
   b. Thing
   c. Undefined
   d. Undefined

56. A _____ is a consumption tax charged at the point of purchase for certain goods and services.
   a. Sales tax0
   b. Thing
   c. Undefined
   d. Undefined

57. A _____ is the part of a fraction that tells how many equal parts make up a whole, and which is used in the name of the fraction: "halves", "thirds", "fourths" or "quarters", "fifths" and so on.
   a. Denominator0
   b. Concept
   c. Undefined
   d. Undefined

58. In mathematics, and in particular in abstract algebra, the _____ is a property of binary operations that generalises the distributive law from elementary algebra.

Chapter 3. Solving Equations and inequalities

   a. Thing
   c. Undefined
   b. Distributive property0
   d. Undefined

59. _____, either of the curved-bracket punctuation marks that together make a set of _____
   a. Parentheses0
   c. Undefined
   b. Thing
   d. Undefined

60. The _____ (symbol _____) and the millibar (symbol mbar, also mb) are units of pressure.
   a. Thing
   c. Undefined
   b. Bar0
   d. Undefined

61. A _____ signifies a point or points of probability on a subject e.g., the _____ of creativity, which allows for the formation of rule or norm or law by interpretation of the phenomena events that can be created.
   a. Thing
   c. Undefined
   b. Principle0
   d. Undefined

62. _____, Greek for "knowledge of nature," is the branch of science concerned with the discovery and characterization of universal laws which govern matter, energy, space, and time.
   a. Physics0
   c. Undefined
   b. Thing
   d. Undefined

63. In physics, _____ is an influence that may cause an object to accelerate. It may be experienced as a lift, a push, or a pull. The actual acceleration of the body is determined by the vector sum of all forces acting on it, known as net _____ or resultant _____.
   a. Thing
   c. Undefined
   b. Force0
   d. Undefined

64. In common philosophical language, a proposition or _____, is the content of an assertion, that is, it is true-or-false and defined by the meaning of a particular piece of language.
   a. Statement0
   c. Undefined
   b. Concept
   d. Undefined

65. A _____ is a number that is less than zero.
   a. Thing
   c. Undefined
   b. Negative number0
   d. Undefined

66. The _____ rule, also known as a slipstick, is a mechanical analog computer, consisting of at least two finely divided scales, most often a fixed outer pair and a movable inner one, with a sliding window called the cursor.
   a. Slide0
   c. Undefined
   b. Thing
   d. Undefined

67. _____ is, or relates to, the _____ temperature scale.
   a. Thing
   c. Undefined
   b. Celsius0
   d. Undefined

68. _____ is a physical property of a system that underlies the common notions of hot and cold; something that is hotter has the greater _____.
   a. Temperature0
   b. Thing
   c. Undefined
   d. Undefined

69. In plane geometry, a _____ is a polygon with four equal sides, four right angles, and parallel opposite sides. In algebra, the _____ of a number is that number multiplied by itself.
   a. Square0
   b. Thing
   c. Undefined
   d. Undefined

70. _____ of an object is its speed in a particular direction.
   a. Velocity0
   b. Thing
   c. Undefined
   d. Undefined

71. Initial objects are also called _____, and terminal objects are also called final.
   a. Thing
   b. Coterminal0
   c. Undefined
   d. Undefined

72. Acid _____ ratio measures the ability of a company to use its near cash or quick assets to immediately extinguish its current liabilities.
   a. Thing
   b. Test0
   c. Undefined
   d. Undefined

73. _____, from Latin meaning "to make progress", is defined in two different ways. Pure economic _____ is the increase in wealth that an investor has from making an investment, taking into consideration all costs associated with that investment including the opportunity cost of capital.
   a. Profit0
   b. Thing
   c. Undefined
   d. Undefined

74. The _____ of measurement are a globally standardized and modernized form of the metric system.
   a. Units0
   b. Thing
   c. Undefined
   d. Undefined

Chapter 3. Solving Equations and inequalities

75. Fixed costs are expenses whose total does not change in proportion to the activity of a business. Unit fixed costs decline with volume following a retangular hyperbola as the volume of production. Variable costs by contrast change in relation to the activity of a business such as sales or production volume. Along with variable costs, fixed costs make up one of the two components of total cost. In the most simple production function total cost is equal to fixed costs plus variable costs. In accounting terminology, fixed costs will broadly include all costs which are not included in cost of goods sold, and variable costs are those captured in costs of goods sold. The implicit assumption required to make the equivalence between the accounting and economics terminology is that the accounting period is equal to the period in which fixed costs do not vary in relation to production. In practice, this equivalence does not always hold and depending on the period under consideration by management, some overhead expenses can be adjusted by management, and the specific allocation of each expense to each category will be decided under cost accounting. In business planning and management accounting, usage of the terms fixed costs, variable costs and others will often differ from usage in economics, and may depend on the intended use. For example, costs may be segregated into per unit costs fixed costs per period, and variable costs as a proportion of revenue. Capital expenditures will usually be allocated separately, and depending on the purpose, a portion may be regularly allocated to expenses as depreciation and amortization and seen as a _____ per period, or the entire amount may be considered upfront fixed costs.
    a. Fixed cost0
    b. Thing
    c. Undefined
    d. Undefined

76. _____ is the application of tools and a processing medium to the transformation of raw materials into finished goods for sale.
    a. Thing
    b. Manufacturing0
    c. Undefined
    d. Undefined

77. A _____ is the part of the dividend that is left over when the dividend is not evenly divisible by the divisor.
    a. Remainder0
    b. Thing
    c. Undefined
    d. Undefined

78. In mathematics, a _____ may be described informally as a number that can be given by an infinite decimal representation.
    a. Thing
    b. Real number0
    c. Undefined
    d. Undefined

79. In mathematics, an _____ is a statement about the relative size or order of two objects.
    a. Thing
    b. Inequality0
    c. Undefined
    d. Undefined

80. An _____ or member of a set is an object that when collected together make up the set.
    a. Thing
    b. Element0
    c. Undefined
    d. Undefined

81. A _____ is a set of possible values that a variable can take on in order to satisfy a given set of conditions, which may include equations and inequalities.
    a. Thing
    b. Solution set0
    c. Undefined
    d. Undefined

Chapter 3. Solving Equations and inequalities

82. A _____ is a one-dimensional picture in which the integers are shown as specially-marked points evenly spaced on a line.
   a. Thing
   b. Number line0
   c. Undefined
   d. Undefined

83. _____ are objects, characters, or other concrete representations of ideas, concepts, or other abstractions.
   a. Thing
   b. Symbols0
   c. Undefined
   d. Undefined

84. The _____ are the only integral domain whose positive elements are well-ordered, and in which order is preserved by addition. Like the natural numbers, the _____ form a countably infinite set. The set of all _____ is usually denoted in mathematics by a boldface Z .
   a. Integers0
   b. Thing
   c. Undefined
   d. Undefined

85. _____ forms part of thinking. Considered the most complex of all intellectual functions, _____ has been defined as higher-order cognitive process that requires the modulation and control of more routine or fundamental skills.
   a. Thing
   b. Problem solving0
   c. Undefined
   d. Undefined

86. In mathematics, a _____ is any one of several different types of functions, mappings, operations, or transformations.
   a. Thing
   b. Projection0
   c. Undefined
   d. Undefined

87. In geometry, a line _____ is a part of a line that is bounded by two end points, and contains every point on the line between its end points.
   a. Concept
   b. Segment0
   c. Undefined
   d. Undefined

88. _____ is change in population over time, and can be quantified as the change in the number of individuals in a population per unit time.
   a. Thing
   b. Population growth0
   c. Undefined
   d. Undefined

89. _____ are activities that are governed by a set of rules or customs and often engaged in competitively.
   a. Thing
   b. Sports0
   c. Undefined
   d. Undefined

90. In mathematics, the _____ of a function is the set of all "output" values produced by that function. Given a function $f : A \to B$, the _____ of f, is defined to be the set $\{x \in B : x = f(a) \text{ for some } a \in A\}$.
   a. Thing
   b. Range0
   c. Undefined
   d. Undefined

91. _____ is a statistical time-series measure of a weighted average of prices of a specified set of goods and services purchased by consumers

Chapter 3. Solving Equations and inequalities

a. Consumer price index0
c. Undefined
b. Thing
d. Undefined

92. The word _____ is used in a variety of ways in mathematics.
a. Thing
b. Index0
c. Undefined
d. Undefined

93. _____ the expected value of a random variable displays the average or central value of the variable. It is a summary value of the distribution of the variable.
a. Thing
b. Determining0
c. Undefined
d. Undefined

94. A _____ is one of the basic shapes of geometry: a polygon with three vertices and three sides which are straight line segments.
a. Triangle0
b. Thing
c. Undefined
d. Undefined

95. A _____ is a function that assigns a number to subsets of a given set.
a. Thing
b. Measure0
c. Undefined
d. Undefined

96. In geometry, a _____ is defined as a quadrilateral where all four of its angles are right angles.
a. Rectangle0
b. Thing
c. Undefined
d. Undefined

97. _____ is the distance around a given two-dimensional object. As a general rule, the _____ of a polygon can always be calculated by adding all the length of the sides together. So, the formula for triangles is P = a + b + c, where a, b and c stand for each side of it. For quadrilaterals the equation is P = a + b + c + d. For equilateral polygons, P = na, where n is the number of sides and a is the side length.
a. Perimeter0
b. Thing
c. Undefined
d. Undefined

98. In mathematics, a _____ function in the sense of algebraic geometry is an everywhere-defined, polynomial function on an algebraic variety V with values in the field K over which V is defined.
a. Regular0
b. Thing
c. Undefined
d. Undefined

99. In finance and economics, _____ is the process of finding the present value of an amount of cash at some future date, and along with compounding cash forms the basis of time value of money calculations.
a. Discount0
b. Thing
c. Undefined
d. Undefined

100. _____ is an adjective usually refering to being in the centre.
a. Thing
b. Central0
c. Undefined
d. Undefined

Chapter 3. Solving Equations and inequalities

101. In set theory and other branches of mathematics, the _____ of a collection of sets is the set that contains everything that belongs to any of the sets, but nothing else.
   a. Thing
   b. Union0
   c. Undefined
   d. Undefined

102. _____ are expenses whose total does not change in proportion to the activity of a business, within the relevant time period or scale of production
   a. Thing
   b. Fixed costs0
   c. Undefined
   d. Undefined

103. In mathematics, a _____ is the end result of a division problem. It can also be expressed as the number of times the divisor divides into the dividend.
   a. Thing
   b. Quotient0
   c. Undefined
   d. Undefined

104. _____ is the technique and science of accurately determining the terrestrial or three-dimensional space position of points and the distances and angles between them.
   a. Thing
   b. Surveying0
   c. Undefined
   d. Undefined

105. In economics, supply and _____ describe market relations between prospective sellers and buyers of a good.
   a. Demand0
   b. Thing
   c. Undefined
   d. Undefined

106. _____ is the production of food, feed, fiber, fuel and other goods by the systematic raizing of plants and animals.
   a. Agriculture0
   b. Thing
   c. Undefined
   d. Undefined

107. The payment of _____ as remuneration for services rendered or products sold is a common way to reward sales people.
   a. Commission0
   b. Thing
   c. Undefined
   d. Undefined

108. Compass and straightedge or ruler-and-compass _____ is the _____ of lengths or angles using only an idealized ruler and compass.
   a. Construction0
   b. Thing
   c. Undefined
   d. Undefined

109. _____ is a term used in accounting, economics and finance with reference to the fact that assets with finite lives lose value over time.
   a. Depreciation0
   b. Thing
   c. Undefined
   d. Undefined

110. _____ is a term used in marketing to indicate how much the price of a product is above the cost of producing and distributing the product.

a. Markup0
c. Undefined

b. Thing
d. Undefined

Chapter 4. Solving Equations and Inequalities: Applications

1. An _____ is a combination of numbers, operators, grouping symbols and/or free variables and bound variables arranged in a meaningful way which can be evaluated..
   - a. Thing
   - b. Expression0
   - c. Undefined
   - d. Undefined

2. _____ is a kind of property which exists as magnitude or multitude. It is among the basic classes of things along with quality, substance, change, and relation.
   - a. Thing
   - b. Amount0
   - c. Undefined
   - d. Undefined

3. A _____ is a symbolic representation denoting a quantity or expression. It often represents an "unknown" quantity that has the potential to change.
   - a. Thing
   - b. Variable0
   - c. Undefined
   - d. Undefined

4. In mathematics and the mathematical sciences, a _____ is a fixed, but possibly unspecified, value. This is in contrast to a variable, which is not fixed.
   - a. Constant0
   - b. Thing
   - c. Undefined
   - d. Undefined

5. A _____ is the result of the addition of a set of numbers. The numbers may be natural numbers, complex numbers, matrices, or still more complicated objects. An infinite _____ is a subtle procedure known as a series.
   - a. Sum0
   - b. Thing
   - c. Undefined
   - d. Undefined

6. _____ is a temperature scale named after the German physicist Daniel Gabriel _____ , who proposed it in 1724.
   - a. Fahrenheit0
   - b. Thing
   - c. Undefined
   - d. Undefined

7. _____ is a physical property of a system that underlies the common notions of hot and cold; something that is hotter has the greater _____.
   - a. Thing
   - b. Temperature0
   - c. Undefined
   - d. Undefined

8. In common philosophical language, a proposition or _____, is the content of an assertion, that is, it is true-or-false and defined by the meaning of a particular piece of language.
   - a. Concept
   - b. Statement0
   - c. Undefined
   - d. Undefined

9. The metre (or _____, see spelling differences) is a measure of length. It is the basic unit of length in the metric system and in the International System of Units (SI), used around the world for general and scientific purposes.
   - a. Concept
   - b. Meter0
   - c. Undefined
   - d. Undefined

Chapter 4. Solving Equations and Inequalities: Applications

10. A _____ is a unit of length, usually used to measure distance, in a number of different systems, including Imperial units, United States customary units and Norwegian/Swedish mil. Its size can vary from system to system, but in each is between 1 and 10 kilometers. In contemporary English contexts _____ refers to either:
   a. Thing
   b. Mile0
   c. Undefined
   d. Undefined

11. _____ is a unit of speed, expressing the number of international miles covered per hour.
   a. Thing
   b. Miles per hour0
   c. Undefined
   d. Undefined

12. _____ are a measure of time.
   a. Minutes0
   b. Thing
   c. Undefined
   d. Undefined

13. In mathematics, a _____ is the result of multiplying, or an expression that identifies factors to be multiplied.
   a. Product0
   b. Thing
   c. Undefined
   d. Undefined

14. _____ is a term used in accounting, economics and finance with reference to the fact that assets with finite lives lose value over time.
   a. Depreciation0
   b. Thing
   c. Undefined
   d. Undefined

15. The State of _____ is a state located in the Rocky Mountain region of the United States of America.
   a. Colorado0
   b. Thing
   c. Undefined
   d. Undefined

16. In economics _____ means before deductions brutto, e.g. _____ domestic or national product, or _____ profit or income
   a. Thing
   b. Gross0
   c. Undefined
   d. Undefined

17. _____ is the production of food, feed, fiber, fuel and other goods by the systematic raizing of plants and animals.
   a. Thing
   b. Agriculture0
   c. Undefined
   d. Undefined

18. The payment of _____ as remuneration for services rendered or products sold is a common way to reward sales people.
   a. Thing
   b. Commission0
   c. Undefined
   d. Undefined

19. The _____ relative to a specified or implied reference level.
   a. Decibel0
   b. Thing
   c. Undefined
   d. Undefined

Chapter 4. Solving Equations and Inequalities: Applications

20. In statistics the _____ of an event i is the number n_i of times the event occurred in the experiment or the study. These frequencies are often graphically represented in histograms.
    a. Frequency0
    b. Concept
    c. Undefined
    d. Undefined

21. In statistics, _____ means the most frequent value assumed by a random variable, or occurring in a sampling of a random variable.
    a. Mode0
    b. Concept
    c. Undefined
    d. Undefined

22. _____ studies and addresses the ways in which individuals, businesses, and organizations raise, allocate, and use monetary resources over time, taking into account the risks entailed in their projects
    a. Finance0
    b. Thing
    c. Undefined
    d. Undefined

23. A _____ is the part of the dividend that is left over when the dividend is not evenly divisible by the divisor.
    a. Remainder0
    b. Thing
    c. Undefined
    d. Undefined

24. In geometry, a _____ is defined as a quadrilateral where all four of its angles are right angles.
    a. Thing
    b. Rectangle0
    c. Undefined
    d. Undefined

25. _____ are activities that are governed by a set of rules or customs and often engaged in competitively.
    a. Thing
    b. Sports0
    c. Undefined
    d. Undefined

26. In plane geometry, a _____ is a polygon with four equal sides, four right angles, and parallel opposite sides. In algebra, the _____ of a number is that number multiplied by itself.
    a. Thing
    b. Square0
    c. Undefined
    d. Undefined

27. _____ is the distance around a given two-dimensional object. As a general rule, the _____ of a polygon can always be calculated by adding all the length of the sides together. So, the formula for triangles is P = a + b + c, where a, b and c stand for each side of it. For quadrilaterals the equation is P = a + b + c + d. For equilateral polygons, P = na, where n is the number of sides and a is the side length.
    a. Thing
    b. Perimeter0
    c. Undefined
    d. Undefined

28. In mathematics, a _____ is an n-tuple with n being 3.
    a. Triple0
    b. Thing
    c. Undefined
    d. Undefined

29. _____ is the transport of people on a trip/journey or the process or time involved in a person or object moving from one location to another.

Chapter 4. Solving Equations and Inequalities: Applications

    a. Travel0   b. Thing
    c. Undefined   d. Undefined

30. A _____ is a special kind of ratio, indicating a relationship between two measurements with different units, such as miles to gallons or cents to pounds.
    a. Rate0   b. Thing
    c. Undefined   d. Undefined

31. A _____ is a compensation which workers receive in exchange for their labor.
    a. Wage0   b. Thing
    c. Undefined   d. Undefined

32. In Euclidean geometry, a uniform _____ is a linear transformation that enlargers or diminishes objects, and whose _____ factor is the same in all directions. This is also called homothethy.
    a. Thing   b. Scale0
    c. Undefined   d. Undefined

33. _____ means in succession or back-to-back
    a. Consecutive0   b. Thing
    c. Undefined   d. Undefined

34. _____ usually refers to money in the form of liquid currency, such as banknotes or coins.
    a. Cash0   b. Thing
    c. Undefined   d. Undefined

35. The _____ are the only integral domain whose positive elements are well-ordered, and in which order is preserved by addition. Like the natural numbers, the _____ form a countably infinite set. The set of all _____ is usually denoted in mathematics by a boldface Z .
    a. Integers0   b. Thing
    c. Undefined   d. Undefined

36. In mathematics, a matrix can be thought of as each row or _____ being a vector. Hence, a space formed by row vectors or _____ vectors are said to be a row space or a _____ space.
    a. Concept   b. Column0
    c. Undefined   d. Undefined

37. In Euclidean geometry, an _____ is a closed segment of a differentiable curve in the two-dimensional plane; for example, a circular _____ is a segment of a circle.
    a. Concept   b. Arc0
    c. Undefined   d. Undefined

38. A _____ of a number is the product of that number with any integer.
    a. Multiple0   b. Thing
    c. Undefined   d. Undefined

Chapter 4. Solving Equations and Inequalities: Applications

39. In mathematics, a _____ is a constant multiplicative factor of a certain object. The object can be such things as a variable, a vector, a function, etc. For example, the _____ of $9x^2$ is 9.
    a. Coefficient0
    b. Thing
    c. Undefined
    d. Undefined

40. A _____ is a negotiable instrument instructing a financial institution to pay a specific amount of a specific currency from a specific demand account held in the maker/depositor's name with that institution. Both the maker and payee may be natural persons or legal entities.
    a. Thing
    b. Check0
    c. Undefined
    d. Undefined

41. _____ the expected value of a random variable displays the average or central value of the variable.It is a summary value of the distribution of the variable.
    a. Thing
    b. Determining0
    c. Undefined
    d. Undefined

42. A _____ is one of the basic shapes of geometry: a polygon with three vertices and three sides which are straight line segments.
    a. Triangle0
    b. Thing
    c. Undefined
    d. Undefined

43. An _____ triange is a triangle with at least two sides of equal length.
    a. Isosceles0
    b. Thing
    c. Undefined
    d. Undefined

44. In geometry, an _____ polygon is a polygon which has all sides of the same length.
    a. Thing
    b. Equilateral0
    c. Undefined
    d. Undefined

45. An _____ is a triangle in which all sides are of equal length.
    a. Equilateral triangle0
    b. Thing
    c. Undefined
    d. Undefined

46. _____ (or proportionality) are two quantities that vary in such a way that one of the quatities is a constant multiple of the other, or equivalently if they have a constant ratio.
    a. Proportions0
    b. Thing
    c. Undefined
    d. Undefined

47. A _____ is a rectangle whose side lengths are in the golden ratio, 1:, that is, approximately 1:1.618.
    a. Golden rectangle0
    b. Thing
    c. Undefined
    d. Undefined

48. In mathematics, and in particular in abstract algebra, the _____ is a property of binary operations that generalises the distributive law from elementary algebra.

a. Distributive property0
b. Thing
c. Undefined
d. Undefined

49. In Euclidean geometry, a _____ is the set of all points in a plane at a fixed distance, called the radius, from a given point, the center.
a. Circle0
b. Thing
c. Undefined
d. Undefined

50. A _____ was a citizen of Babylonia, named for its capital city, Babylon, which was an ancient state in the south part of Mesopotamia (in modern Iraq), combining the territories of Sumer and Akkad.
a. Babylonian0
b. Place
c. Undefined
d. Undefined

51. In mathematics, a _____ of an integer n, also called a factor of n, is an integer which evenly divides n without leaving a remainder.
a. Divisor0
b. Thing
c. Undefined
d. Undefined

52. A _____ is a function that assigns a number to subsets of a given set.
a. Thing
b. Measure0
c. Undefined
d. Undefined

53. Angles smaller than a right angle are called _____ angles (less than 90 degrees).
a. Acute0
b. Concept
c. Undefined
d. Undefined

54. Any angle larger than 90 degrees and less than 180 degrees, is called an _____ angle.
a. Concept
b. Obtuse0
c. Undefined
d. Undefined

55. A pair of angles are _____ if the sum of their angles is 90°.
a. Complementary0
b. Concept
c. Undefined
d. Undefined

56. A pair of angles is _____ if their respective measures sum to 180 degrees.
a. Concept
b. Supplementary0
c. Undefined
d. Undefined

57. In set theory and other branches of mathematics, two kinds of complements are defined, the relative _____ and the absolute _____.
a. Complement0
b. Thing
c. Undefined
d. Undefined

58. In geometry, two lines or planes if one falls on the other in such a way as to create congruent adjacent angles. The term may be used as a noun or adjective. Thus, referring to Figure 1, the line AB is the _____ to CD through the point B.

Chapter 4. Solving Equations and Inequalities: Applications 41

   a. Thing
   c. Undefined
   b. Perpendicular0
   d. Undefined

59. In geometry and trigonometry, a _____ is defined as an angle between two straight intersecting lines of ninety degrees, or one-quarter of a circle.
   a. Thing
   c. Undefined
   b. Right angle0
   d. Undefined

60. In geometry, _____ lines are two lines that share one or more common points.
   a. Thing
   c. Undefined
   b. Intersecting0
   d. Undefined

61. In mathematics, the additive inverse, or _____ of a number n is the number that, when added to n, yields zero. The additive inverse of n is denoted −n. For example, 7 is −7, because 7 + (−7) = 0, and the additive inverse of −0.3 is 0.3, because −0.3 + 0.3 = 0.
   a. Opposite0
   c. Undefined
   b. Thing
   d. Undefined

62. In mathematics, the _____ of a number n is the number that, when added to n, yields zero. The _____ of n is denoted −n. For example, 7 is −7, because 7 + (−7) = 0, and the _____ of −0.3 is 0.3, because −0.3 + 0.3 = 0.
   a. Thing
   c. Undefined
   b. Additive inverse0
   d. Undefined

63. A pair of angles are said to be _____ if they share the same vertex and are bounded by the same pair of lines but are opposite to each other. They are also congruent.
   a. Thing
   c. Undefined
   b. Vertical angles0
   d. Undefined

64. In mathematics, the _____ of two sets A and B is the set that contains all elements of A that also belong to B (or equivalently, all elements of B that also belong to A), but no other elements.
   a. Thing
   c. Undefined
   b. Intersection0
   d. Undefined

65. In geometry, _____ angles are angles that have a common ray coming out of the vertex going between two other rays.
   a. Adjacent0
   c. Undefined
   b. Concept
   d. Undefined

66. In combinatorial mathematics, given a collection C of disjoint sets, a _____ is a set containing exactly one element from each member of the collection: it is a section of the quotient map induced by the collection.
   a. Thing
   c. Undefined
   b. Transversal0
   d. Undefined

67. The existence and properties of _____ are the basis of Euclid's parallel postulate. _____ are two lines on the same plane that do not intersect even assuming that lines extend to infinity in either direction.

a. Parallel lines0
b. Thing
c. Undefined
d. Undefined

68. An _____ is an angle formed by two sides of a simple polygon that share an endpoint, namely, the angle on the inner side of the polygon.
   a. Thing
   b. Interior angle0
   c. Undefined
   d. Undefined

69. In geometry, a line _____ is a part of a line that is bounded by two end points, and contains every point on the line between its end points.
   a. Segment0
   b. Concept
   c. Undefined
   d. Undefined

70. A _____ is a part of a line that is bounded by two end points, and contains every point on the line between its end points.
   a. Line segment0
   b. Thing
   c. Undefined
   d. Undefined

71. _____ has one 90° internal angle a right angle.
   a. Right triangle0
   b. Thing
   c. Undefined
   d. Undefined

72. In mathematics, there are several meanings of _____ depending on the subject.
   a. Thing
   b. Degree0
   c. Undefined
   d. Undefined

73. In mathematics, science including computer science, linguistics and engineering, an _____ is, generally speaking, an independent variable or input to a function.
   a. Argument0
   b. Thing
   c. Undefined
   d. Undefined

74. _____ is the estimation of a physical quantity such as distance, energy, temperature, or time.
   a. Measurement0
   b. Thing
   c. Undefined
   d. Undefined

75. In mathematics a _____ is a function which defines a distance between elements of a set.
   a. Thing
   b. Metric0
   c. Undefined
   d. Undefined

76. The _____ is a decimalized system of measurement based on the metre and the gram.
   a. Concept
   b. Metric system0
   c. Undefined
   d. Undefined

77. _____ is the art and science of designing buildings and structures.

Chapter 4. Solving Equations and Inequalities: Applications

a. Thing
b. Architecture0
c. Undefined
d. Undefined

78. _____ is a term used in marketing to indicate how much the price of a product is above the cost of producing and distributing the product.
a. Thing
b. Markup0
c. Undefined
d. Undefined

79. In finance and economics, _____ is the process of finding the present value of an amount of cash at some future date, and along with compounding cash forms the basis of time value of money calculations.
a. Discount0
b. Thing
c. Undefined
d. Undefined

80. _____ is a way of expressing a number as a fraction of 100 per cent meaning "per hundred".
a. Percent0
b. Thing
c. Undefined
d. Undefined

81. In mathematics, a _____ function in the sense of algebraic geometry is an everywhere-defined, polynomial function on an algebraic variety V with values in the field K over which V is defined.
a. Regular0
b. Thing
c. Undefined
d. Undefined

82. The _____ is different from a more normal interest rate.
a. Thing
b. Discount rate0
c. Undefined
d. Undefined

83. A _____ is a craftsman who creates jewelry using jewels, precious metals, or other substances.
a. Jeweler0
b. Thing
c. Undefined
d. Undefined

84. In mathematics, a _____ is an algebraic structure in which addition and multiplication are defined and have properties listed below.
a. Ring0
b. Thing
c. Undefined
d. Undefined

85. In mathematics, a subset of Euclidean space R^n is called _____ if it is closed and bounded.
a. Thing
b. Compact0
c. Undefined
d. Undefined

86. _____ is a lightweight markup language, originally created by John Gruber and Aaron Swartz, which aims for maximum readability and "publishability" of both its input and output forms, taking many cues from existing conventions for marking up plain text in email.
a. Markdown0
b. Thing
c. Undefined
d. Undefined

Chapter 4. Solving Equations and Inequalities: Applications

87. In mathematics, a _____ can mean either an element of the set {1, 2, 3, ...} (i.e the positive integers) or an element of the set {0, 1, 2, 3, ...} (i.e. the non-negative integers).
   a. Whole number0
   b. Concept
   c. Undefined
   d. Undefined

88. _____ are payments to distribution channel members for performing some function .
   a. Thing
   b. Trade discounts0
   c. Undefined
   d. Undefined

89. A _____ is the sum of the elements of a sequence.
   a. Thing
   b. Series0
   c. Undefined
   d. Undefined

90. _____ is the fee paid on borrowed money.
   a. Thing
   b. Interest0
   c. Undefined
   d. Undefined

91. An _____ is the fee paid on borrow money.
   a. Concept
   b. Interest rate0
   c. Undefined
   d. Undefined

92. _____ or investing is a term with several closely-related meanings in business management, finance and economics, related to saving or deferring consumption.
   a. Investment0
   b. Thing
   c. Undefined
   d. Undefined

93. _____ finance, in finance, a debt security, issued by Issuer
   a. Thing
   b. Bond0
   c. Undefined
   d. Undefined

94. A _____ or CD is a time deposit, a financial product commonly offered to consumers by banks, thrift institutions, and credit unions.
   a. Certificate of deposit0
   b. Thing
   c. Undefined
   d. Undefined

95. The _____, the average in everyday English, which is also called the arithmetic _____ (and is distinguished from the geometric _____ or harmonic _____). The average is also called the sample _____. The expected value of a random variable, which is also called the population _____.
   a. Thing
   b. Mean0
   c. Undefined
   d. Undefined

96. A _____ is a form of collective investment that pools money from many investors and invests their money in stocks, bonds, short-term money market instruments, and/or other securities.
   a. Mutual fund0
   b. Thing
   c. Undefined
   d. Undefined

Chapter 4. Solving Equations and Inequalities: Applications

97. _____ is a payment made by a company to its shareholders
   - a. Thing
   - b. Dividend0
   - c. Undefined
   - d. Undefined

98. _____ interest refers to the fact that whenever interest is calculated, it is based not only on the original principal, but also on any unpaid interest that has been added to the principal.
   - a. Compound0
   - b. Thing
   - c. Undefined
   - d. Undefined

99. In chemistry, a _____ is substance made by combining two or more different materials in such a way that no chemical reaction occurs.
   - a. Mixture0
   - b. Thing
   - c. Undefined
   - d. Undefined

100. In mathematics, an inequality is a statement about the relative size or order of two objects. For example 14 > 10, or 14 is _____ 10.
   - a. Thing
   - b. Greater than0
   - c. Undefined
   - d. Undefined

101. The _____ or kilogramme is the SI base unit of mass. It is defined as being equal to the mass of the international prototype of the _____.
   - a. Kilogram0
   - b. Thing
   - c. Undefined
   - d. Undefined

102. U.S. liquid _____ is legally defined as 231 cubic inches, and is equal to 3.785411784 litres or abotu 0.13368 cubic feet. This is the most common definition of a _____. The U.S. fluid ounce is defined as 1/128 of a U.S. _____.
   - a. Thing
   - b. Gallon0
   - c. Undefined
   - d. Undefined

103. _____ is an adjective usually refering to being in the centre.
   - a. Thing
   - b. Central0
   - c. Undefined
   - d. Undefined

104. In botany, _____ are above-ground plant organs specialized for photosynthesis. Their characteristics are typically analyzed by using Fiobonacci's sequences.
   - a. Thing
   - b. Leaves0
   - c. Undefined
   - d. Undefined

105. _____, in economics and political economy, are the distributions or payments awarded to the various suppliers of the factors of production.
   - a. Thing
   - b. Returns0
   - c. Undefined
   - d. Undefined

106. In mathematics, a _____ is a two-dimensional manifold or surface that is perfectly flat.

a. Thing
c. Undefined
b. Plane0
d. Undefined

107. In mathematics, _____ are two-dimensional manifolds or surfaces that are perfectly flat.
a. Thing
c. Undefined
b. Planes0
d. Undefined

108. In mathematics, an _____, mean, or central tendency of a data set refers to a measure of the "middle" or "expected" value of the data set.
a. Average0
c. Undefined
b. Concept
d. Undefined

109. _____ are objects, characters, or other concrete representations of ideas, concepts, or other abstractions.
a. Symbols0
c. Undefined
b. Thing
d. Undefined

110. In mathematics, an _____ is a statement about the relative size or order of two objects.
a. Thing
c. Undefined
b. Inequality0
d. Undefined

111. In mathematics, _____ are essentially word problems that are designed to use mathematical critical thinking in everyday situations.
a. Thing
c. Undefined
b. Application problems0
d. Undefined

112. Acid _____ ratio measures the ability of a company to use its near cash or quick assets to immediately extinguish its current liabilities.
a. Test0
c. Undefined
b. Thing
d. Undefined

113. _____, from Latin meaning "to make progress", is defined in two different ways. Pure economic _____ is the increase in wealth that an investor has from making an investment, taking into consideration all costs associated with that investment including the opportunity cost of capital.
a. Thing
c. Undefined
b. Profit0
d. Undefined

114. The _____ of measurement are a globally standardized and modernized form of the metric system.
a. Thing
c. Undefined
b. Units0
d. Undefined

115. _____ is the level of functional and/or metabolic efficiency of an organism at both the micro level.
a. Thing
c. Undefined
b. Health0
d. Undefined

116. _____ is a form of periodic payment from an employer to an employee, which is specified in an employment contract.

Chapter 4. Solving Equations and Inequalities: Applications

a. Gross pay0
c. Undefined
b. Thing
d. Undefined

117. A _____ is a form of periodic payment from an employer to an employee, which is specified in an employment contract.
    a. Thing
    b. Salary0
    c. Undefined
    d. Undefined

118. A _____ is a fee added to a customer's bill.
    a. Service charge0
    b. Thing
    c. Undefined
    d. Undefined

119. Initial objects are also called _____, and terminal objects are also called final.
    a. Coterminal0
    b. Thing
    c. Undefined
    d. Undefined

120. A _____ is a method of using property as security for the payment of a debt.
    a. Mortgage0
    b. Thing
    c. Undefined
    d. Undefined

121. A _____ is a type of debt. All material things can be lent but this article focuses exclusively on monetary loans. Like all debt instruments, a _____ entails the redistribution of financial assets over time, between the lender and the borrower.
    a. Thing
    b. Loan0
    c. Undefined
    d. Undefined

122. In the scientific method, an _____ (Latin: ex-+-periri, "of (or from) trying"), is a set of actions and observations, performed in the context of solving a particular problem or question, in order to support or falsify a hypothesis or research concerning phenomena.
    a. Experiment0
    b. Thing
    c. Undefined
    d. Undefined

123. In mathematics, defined and _____ are used to explain whether or not expressions have meaningful, sensible, and unambiguous values.
    a. Thing
    b. Undefined0
    c. Undefined
    d. Undefined

124. In mathematics, the multiplicative inverse of a number x, denoted 1/x or x^{-1}, is the number which, when multiplied by x, yields 1. The multiplicative inverse of x is also called the _____ of x.
    a. Reciprocal0
    b. Thing
    c. Undefined
    d. Undefined

125. In mathematics, _____ is an elementary arithmetic operation. When one of the numbers is a whole number, _____ is the repeated sum of the other number.

a. Multiplication0 b. Thing
c. Undefined d. Undefined

126. A _____ is a number that is less than zero.
a. Thing b. Negative number0
c. Undefined d. Undefined

127. _____ forms part of thinking. Considered the most complex of all intellectual functions, _____ has been defined as higher-order cognitive process that requires the modulation and control of more routine or fundamental skills.
a. Thing b. Problem solving0
c. Undefined d. Undefined

128. A _____ is a simplified and structured visual representation of concepts, ideas, constructions, relations, statistical data, anatomy etc used in all aspects of human activities to visualize and clarify the topic.
a. Thing b. Diagram0
c. Undefined d. Undefined

129. _____ is the mathematical action of repeatedly adding or subtracting one, usually to find out how many objects there are or to set aside a desired number of objects.
a. Counting0 b. Thing
c. Undefined d. Undefined

130. In Graph theory, a _____ is a digraph with weighted edges.
a. Network0 b. Concept
c. Undefined d. Undefined

131. In mathematics, a _____ number (or a _____) is a natural number that has exactly two (distinct) natural number divisors, which are 1 and the _____ number itself.
a. Thing b. Prime0
c. Undefined d. Undefined

132. _____ is a mathematical science pertaining to the collection, analysis, interpretation or explanation, and presentation of data. It is applicable to a wide variety of academic disciplines, from the physical and social sciences to the humanities.
a. Thing b. Statistics0
c. Undefined d. Undefined

133. In mathematics, the conjugate _____ or adjoint matrix of an m-by-n matrix A with complex entries is the n-by-m matrix A* obtained from A by taking the transpose and then taking the complex conjugate of each entry.
a. Thing b. Pairs0
c. Undefined d. Undefined

134. When _____ symmetry one can determine whether or not an object is symmetric with respect to a given mathematical operation, if, when applied to the object, this operation does not change the object or its appearance.

Chapter 4. Solving Equations and Inequalities: Applications

a. Investigating0
c. Undefined
b. Thing
d. Undefined

135. In geometry, the _____ of an object is a point in some sense in the middle of the object.
a. Thing
c. Undefined
b. Center0
d. Undefined

136. _____ is the design, analysis, and/or construction of works for practical purposes.
a. Engineering0
c. Undefined
b. Thing
d. Undefined

137. _____ is a retirement plan account that provides some tax advantages for retirement savings in the United States.
a. Individual Retirement Account0
c. Undefined
b. Thing
d. Undefined

138. _____ is the value of a coin or paper money, as printed on the coin or bill itself by the minting authority.
a. Face value0
c. Undefined
b. Concept
d. Undefined

139. In mathematics, _____ geometry was the traditional name for the geometry of three-dimensional Euclidean space — for practical purposes the kind of space we live in.
a. Thing
c. Undefined
b. Solid0
d. Undefined

140. A _____ is a set of possible values that a variable can take on in order to satisfy a given set of conditions, which may include equations and inequalities.
a. Thing
c. Undefined
b. Solution set0
d. Undefined

141. In sociology and biology a _____ is the collection of people or organisms of a particular species living in a given geographic area or space, usually measured by a census.
a. Population0
c. Undefined
b. Thing
d. Undefined

142. _____ is change in population over time, and can be quantified as the change in the number of individuals in a population per unit time.
a. Thing
c. Undefined
b. Population growth0
d. Undefined

143. In mathematics, a _____ is a countable collection of open covers of a topological space that satisfies certain separation axioms.
a. Development0
c. Undefined
b. Thing
d. Undefined

Chapter 4. Solving Equations and Inequalities: Applications

144. Compass and straightedge or ruler-and-compass _____ is the _____ of lengths or angles using only an idealized ruler and compass.
  a. Thing
  b. Construction0
  c. Undefined
  d. Undefined

145. _____, or Fuel efficiency can sometimes mean the same as thermal efficiency, that is, the efficiency of converting energy contained in a carrier fuel to kinetic energy or work.
  a. Fuel consumption0
  b. Thing
  c. Undefined
  d. Undefined

146. _____ are the basic objects of study in graph theory. Informally speaking, a graph is a set of objects called points, nodes, or vertices connected by links called lines or edges.
  a. Thing
  b. Graphs0
  c. Undefined
  d. Undefined

147. _____ is a statistical measure of the average length of survival of a living thing.
  a. Life expectancy0
  b. Thing
  c. Undefined
  d. Undefined

148. _____ is the application of tools and a processing medium to the transformation of raw materials into finished goods for sale.
  a. Manufacturing0
  b. Thing
  c. Undefined
  d. Undefined

Chapter 5. Linear Equations and inequalities

1. A _____ is a set of numbers that designate location in a given reference system, such as x,y in a planar _____ system or an x,y,z in a three-dimensional _____ system.
   a. Coordinate0
   b. Thing
   c. Undefined
   d. Undefined

2. In mathematics and its applications, a _____ is a system for assigning an n-tuple of numbers or scalars to each point in an n-dimensional space.
   a. Concept
   b. Coordinate system0
   c. Undefined
   d. Undefined

3. _____ is a branch of mathematics concerning the study of structure, relation and quantity.
   a. Concept
   b. Algebra0
   c. Undefined
   d. Undefined

4. _____ is the study of geometry using the principles of algebra. _____ can be explained more simply: it is concerned with defining geometrical shapes in a numerical way and extracting numerical information from that representation.
   a. Thing
   b. Analytic geometry0
   c. Undefined
   d. Undefined

5. _____ was a highly influential French philosopher, mathematician, scientist, and writer. Dubbed the "Founder of Modern Philosophy", and the "Father of Modern Mathematics". His theories provided the basis for the calculus of Newton and Leibniz, by applying infinitesimal calculus to the tangent line problem, thus permitting the evolution of that branch of modern mathematics
   a. Descartes0
   b. Person
   c. Undefined
   d. Undefined

6. In mathematics, the _____ of a coordinate system is the point where the axes of the system intersect.
   a. Origin0
   b. Thing
   c. Undefined
   d. Undefined

7. In astronomy, geography, geometry and related sciences and contexts, a plane is said to be _____ at a given point if it is locally perpendicular to the gradient of the gravity field, i.e., with the direction of the gravitational force at that point.
   a. Horizontal0
   b. Thing
   c. Undefined
   d. Undefined

8. In mathematics, the _____ of two sets A and B is the set that contains all elements of A that also belong to B (or equivalently, all elements of B that also belong to A), but no other elements.
   a. Thing
   b. Intersection0
   c. Undefined
   d. Undefined

9. An _____ is when two lines intersect somewhere on a plane creating a right angle at intersection
   a. Axes0
   b. Thing
   c. Undefined
   d. Undefined

10. An _____ is a straight line around which a geometric figure can be rotated.

a. Axis0
b. Thing
c. Undefined
d. Undefined

11. In mathematics, a _____ is a two-dimensional manifold or surface that is perfectly flat.
   a. Thing
   b. Plane0
   c. Undefined
   d. Undefined

12. A _____ consists of one quarter of the coordinate plane.
   a. Quadrant0
   b. Thing
   c. Undefined
   d. Undefined

13. An _____ is a collection of two not necessarily distinct objects, one of which is distinguished as the first coordinate and the other as the second coordinate.
   a. Ordered pair0
   b. Thing
   c. Undefined
   d. Undefined

14. The _____ of measurement are a globally standardized and modernized form of the metric system.
   a. Thing
   b. Units0
   c. Undefined
   d. Undefined

15. _____ are the basic objects of study in graph theory. Informally speaking, a graph is a set of objects called points, nodes, or vertices connected by links called lines or edges.
   a. Thing
   b. Graphs0
   c. Undefined
   d. Undefined

16. In mathematics, the conjugate _____ or adjoint matrix of an m-by-n matrix A with complex entries is the n-by-m matrix A* obtained from A by taking the transpose and then taking the complex conjugate of each entry.
   a. Thing
   b. Pairs0
   c. Undefined
   d. Undefined

17. The _____ are the only integral domain whose positive elements are well-ordered, and in which order is preserved by addition. Like the natural numbers, the _____ form a countably infinite set. The set of all _____ is usually denoted in mathematics by a boldface Z .
   a. Thing
   b. Integers0
   c. Undefined
   d. Undefined

18. A _____ is a symbolic representation denoting a quantity or expression. It often represents an "unknown" quantity that has the potential to change.
   a. Thing
   b. Variable0
   c. Undefined
   d. Undefined

19. _____ is the fee paid on borrowed money.
   a. Thing
   b. Interest0
   c. Undefined
   d. Undefined

Chapter 5. Linear Equations and inequalities

20. A _____ is a simplified and structured visual representation of concepts, ideas, constructions, relations, statistical data, anatomy etc used in all aspects of human activities to visualize and clarify the topic.
a. Thing
b. Diagram0
c. Undefined
d. Undefined

21. _____ is a mathematical science pertaining to the collection, analysis, interpretation or explanation, and presentation of data. It is applicable to a wide variety of academic disciplines, from the physical and social sciences to the humanities.
a. Thing
b. Statistics0
c. Undefined
d. Undefined

22. The _____, the average in everyday English, which is also called the arithmetic _____ (and is distinguished from the geometric _____ or harmonic _____). The average is also called the sample _____. The expected value of a random variable, which is also called the population _____.
a. Mean0
b. Thing
c. Undefined
d. Undefined

23. _____ is a synonym for information.
a. Data0
b. Thing
c. Undefined
d. Undefined

24. A _____ is a special kind of ratio, indicating a relationship between two measurements with different units, such as miles to gallons or cents to pounds.
a. Rate0
b. Thing
c. Undefined
d. Undefined

25. A _____ is a function that assigns a number to subsets of a given set.
a. Measure0
b. Thing
c. Undefined
d. Undefined

26. Acid _____ ratio measures the ability of a company to use its near cash or quick assets to immediately extinguish its current liabilities.
a. Thing
b. Test0
c. Undefined
d. Undefined

27. The metre (or _____, see spelling differences) is a measure of length. It is the basic unit of length in the metric system and in the International System of Units (SI), used around the world for general and scientific purposes.
a. Concept
b. Meter0
c. Undefined
d. Undefined

28. In business, particularly accounting, a _____ is the time intervals that the accounts, statement, payments, or other calculations cover.
a. Period0
b. Thing
c. Undefined
d. Undefined

Chapter 5. Linear Equations and inequalities

29. In sociology and biology a _____ is the collection of people or organisms of a particular species living in a given geographic area or space, usually measured by a census.
    a. Population0
    b. Thing
    c. Undefined
    d. Undefined

30. In mathematics, an _____, mean, or central tendency of a data set refers to a measure of the "middle" or "expected" value of the data set.
    a. Average0
    b. Concept
    c. Undefined
    d. Undefined

31. In mathematics and the mathematical sciences, a _____ is a fixed, but possibly unspecified, value. This is in contrast to a variable, which is not fixed.
    a. Thing
    b. Constant0
    c. Undefined
    d. Undefined

32. In elementary algebra, an _____ is a set that contains every real number between two indicated numbers and may contain the two numbers themselves.
    a. Interval0
    b. Thing
    c. Undefined
    d. Undefined

33. In common philosophical language, a proposition or _____, is the content of an assertion, that is, it is true-or-false and defined by the meaning of a particular piece of language.
    a. Concept
    b. Statement0
    c. Undefined
    d. Undefined

34. The _____ is the y- coordinate of a point within a two dimensional coordinate system. It is sometimes used to refer to the axis rather than the distance along the coordinate system.
    a. Thing
    b. Ordinate0
    c. Undefined
    d. Undefined

35. _____, or Fuel efficiency can sometimes mean the same as thermal efficiency, that is, the efficiency of converting energy contained in a carrier fuel to kinetic energy or work.
    a. Fuel use0
    b. Thing
    c. Undefined
    d. Undefined

36. _____ are activities that are governed by a set of rules or customs and often engaged in competitively.
    a. Thing
    b. Sports0
    c. Undefined
    d. Undefined

37. _____ is a physical property of a system that underlies the common notions of hot and cold; something that is hotter has the greater _____.
    a. Temperature0
    b. Thing
    c. Undefined
    d. Undefined

Chapter 5. Linear Equations and inequalities

38. _____, usually denoted symbolically by the Greek letter phi, ϕ, gives the location of a place on Earth north or south of the equator. _____ is an angular measurement in degrees (marked with °) ranging from 0° at the Equator (low _____) to 90° at the poles (90° N for the North Pole or 90° S for the South Pole; high _____). The complementary angle of a _____ is called the colatitude.
 a. Thing
 b. Latitude0
 c. Undefined
 d. Undefined

39. _____ describes the location of a place on Earth east or west of a north-south line called the Prime Meridian.
 a. Longitude0
 b. Thing
 c. Undefined
 d. Undefined

40. In mathematics, a _____ is a constant multiplicative factor of a certain object. The object can be such things as a variable, a vector, a function, etc. For example, the _____ of $9x^2$ is 9.
 a. Coefficient0
 b. Thing
 c. Undefined
 d. Undefined

41. The word _____ comes from the Latin word linearis, which means created by lines.
 a. Thing
 b. Linear0
 c. Undefined
 d. Undefined

42. A _____ is an equation in which each term is either a constant or the product of a constant times the first power of a variable.
 a. Linear equation0
 b. Thing
 c. Undefined
 d. Undefined

43. _____ or arithmetics is the oldest and most elementary branch of mathematics, used by almost everyone, for tasks ranging from simple daily counting to advanced science and business calculations.
 a. Thing
 b. Arithmetic0
 c. Undefined
 d. Undefined

44. In linear algebra, the _____ of an n-by-n square matrix A is defined to be the sum of the elements on the main diagonal of A,
 a. Thing
 b. Trace0
 c. Undefined
 d. Undefined

45. In mathematics, _____ is an elementary arithmetic operation. When one of the numbers is a whole number, _____ is the repeated sum of the other number.
 a. Multiplication0
 b. Thing
 c. Undefined
 d. Undefined

46. In mathematics, the multiplicative inverse of a number x, denoted $1/x$ or x^{-1}, is the number which, when multiplied by x, yields 1. The multiplicative inverse of x is also called the _____ of x.
 a. Reciprocal0
 b. Thing
 c. Undefined
 d. Undefined

Chapter 5. Linear Equations and inequalities

47. In mathematics, and in particular in abstract algebra, the _____ is a property of binary operations that generalises the distributive law from elementary algebra.
    a. Distributive property0
    b. Thing
    c. Undefined
    d. Undefined

48. In mathematics, _____ expressions is used to reduce the expression into the lowest possible term.
    a. Thing
    b. Simplifying0
    c. Undefined
    d. Undefined

49. Any point where a graph makes contact with an coordinate axis is called an _____ of the graph
    a. Thing
    b. Intercept0
    c. Undefined
    d. Undefined

50. _____ is often used to describe the measurement of the steepness, incline, gradient, or grade of a straight line. The _____ is defined as the ratio of the "rise" divided by the "run" between two points on a line, or in other words, the ratio of the altitude change to the horizontal distance between any two points on the line.
    a. Thing
    b. Slope0
    c. Undefined
    d. Undefined

51. A _____ is a quantity that denotes the proportional amount or magnitude of one quantity relative to another.
    a. Thing
    b. Ratio0
    c. Undefined
    d. Undefined

52. A _____ is a number that is less than zero.
    a. Thing
    b. Negative number0
    c. Undefined
    d. Undefined

53. A _____ is the part of a fraction that tells how many equal parts make up a whole, and which is used in the name of the fraction: "halves", "thirds", "fourths" or "quarters", "fifths" and so on.
    a. Concept
    b. Denominator0
    c. Undefined
    d. Undefined

54. In mathematics, defined and _____ are used to explain whether or not expressions have meaningful, sensible, and unambiguous values.
    a. Thing
    b. Undefined0
    c. Undefined
    d. Undefined

55. The existence and properties of _____ are the basis of Euclid's parallel postulate. _____ are two lines on the same plane that do not intersect even assuming that lines extend to infinity in either direction.
    a. Parallel lines0
    b. Thing
    c. Undefined
    d. Undefined

56. In geometry, an _____ of a triangle is a straight line through a vertex and perpendicular to (i.e. forming a right angle with) the opposite side or an extension of the opposite side.

Chapter 5. Linear Equations and inequalities

a. Altitude0
b. Concept
c. Undefined
d. Undefined

57. _____ are a measure of time.
a. Thing
b. Minutes0
c. Undefined
d. Undefined

58. _____ is a fixed, but possibly unspecified, value. This is in contrast to a variable, which is not fixed.
a. Constant term0
b. Thing
c. Undefined
d. Undefined

59. _____ is the level of functional and/or metabolic efficiency of an organism at both the micro level.
a. Health0
b. Thing
c. Undefined
d. Undefined

60. A _____ is a unit of length, usually used to measure distance, in a number of different systems, including Imperial units, United States customary units and Norwegian/Swedish mil. Its size can vary from system to system, but in each is between 1 and 10 kilometers. In contemporary English contexts _____ refers to either:
a. Mile0
b. Thing
c. Undefined
d. Undefined

61. _____ is a temperature scale named after the German physicist Daniel Gabriel _____ , who proposed it in 1724.
a. Fahrenheit0
b. Thing
c. Undefined
d. Undefined

62. _____ is, or relates to, the _____ temperature scale .
a. Celsius0
b. Thing
c. Undefined
d. Undefined

63. An _____ or member of a set is an object that when collected together make up the set.
a. Element0
b. Thing
c. Undefined
d. Undefined

64. In mathematics, the _____ , or members of a set or more generally a class are all those objects which when collected together make up the set or class.
a. Thing
b. Elements0
c. Undefined
d. Undefined

65. A _____, as defined by the International Astronomical Union , is a celestial body orbiting a star or stellar remnant that is massive enough to be rounded by its own gravity, not massive enough to cause thermonuclear fusion in its core, and has cleared its neighboring region of planetesimals.
a. Planet0
b. Thing
c. Undefined
d. Undefined

Chapter 5. Linear Equations and inequalities

66. In mathematics, a _____ of a k-place relation $L \subseteq X_1 \times ... \times X_k$ is one of the sets X_j, $1 \le j \le k$. In the special case where k = 2 and $L \subseteq X_1 \times X_2$ is a function $L : X_1 \to X_2$, it is conventional to refer to X_1 as the _____ of the function and to refer to X_2 as the codomain of the function.
   a. Domain0
   b. Thing
   c. Undefined
   d. Undefined

67. In mathematics, the _____ of a function is the set of all "output" values produced by that function. Given a function $f : A \to B$, the _____ of f, is defined to be the set $\{x \in B : x = f(a)$ for some $a \in A\}$.
   a. Thing
   b. Range0
   c. Undefined
   d. Undefined

68. The mathematical concept of a _____ expresses the intuitive idea of deterministic dependence between two quantities, one of which is viewed as primary and the other as secondary. A _____ then is a way to associate a unique output for each input of a specified type, for example, a real number or an element of a given set.
   a. Thing
   b. Function0
   c. Undefined
   d. Undefined

69. In mathematics, in the field of group theory, a _____ of a group is a quasisimple subnormal subgroup.
   a. Concept
   b. Component0
   c. Undefined
   d. Undefined

70. In mathematics, a _____ may be described informally as a number that can be given by an infinite decimal representation.
   a. Real number0
   b. Thing
   c. Undefined
   d. Undefined

71. In plane geometry, a _____ is a polygon with four equal sides, four right angles, and parallel opposite sides. In algebra, the _____ of a number is that number multiplied by itself.
   a. Thing
   b. Square0
   c. Undefined
   d. Undefined

72. An _____ is a combination of numbers, operators, grouping symbols and/or free variables and bound variables arranged in a meaningful way which can be evaluated..
   a. Expression0
   b. Thing
   c. Undefined
   d. Undefined

73. Mathematical _____ is used to represent ideas.
   a. Thing
   b. Notation0
   c. Undefined
   d. Undefined

74. In a function the _____, is the variable which is the value, i.e. the "output", of the function.
   a. Dependent variable0
   b. Thing
   c. Undefined
   d. Undefined

75. In mathematics, an _____ is any of the arguments, i.e. "inputs", to a function. Thus if we have a function f(x), then x is a _____.

Chapter 5. Linear Equations and inequalities

a. Thing
c. Undefined
b. Independent variable0
d. Undefined

76. In mathematics, the _____ f is the collection of all ordered pairs . In particular, graph means the graphical representation of this collection, in the form of a curve or surface, together with axes, etc. Graphing on a Cartesian plane is sometimes referred to as curve sketching.
a. Graph of a function0
c. Undefined
b. Thing
d. Undefined

77. In mathematics, the term _____ is applied to certain functions. There are two common ways it is applied: these are related historically, but diverged somewhat during the twentieth century.
a. Thing
c. Undefined
b. Functional0
d. Undefined

78. A _____ is a first degree polynomial mathematical function of the form: f(x) = mx + b where m and b are real constants and x is a real variable.
a. Linear function0
c. Undefined
b. Thing
d. Undefined

79. _____ is a kind of property which exists as magnitude or multitude. It is among the basic classes of things along with quality, substance, change, and relation.
a. Amount0
c. Undefined
b. Thing
d. Undefined

80. An _____ is the fee paid on borrow money.
a. Concept
c. Undefined
b. Interest rate0
d. Undefined

81. _____ or investing is a term with several closely-related meanings in business management, finance and economics, related to saving or deferring consumption.
a. Thing
c. Undefined
b. Investment0
d. Undefined

82. _____ is the transport of people on a trip/journey or the process or time involved in a person or object moving from one location to another.
a. Thing
c. Undefined
b. Travel0
d. Undefined

83. _____ is a term used in accounting, economics and finance with reference to the fact that assets with finite lives lose value over time.
a. Depreciation0
c. Undefined
b. Thing
d. Undefined

84. In geometry, the relations of _____ are those such as 'lies on' between points and lines (as in 'point P lies on line L'), and 'intersects' (as in 'line L_1 intersects line L_2', in three-dimensional space). That is, they are the binary relations describing how subsets meet.

Chapter 5. Linear Equations and inequalities

a. Incidence0
b. Thing
c. Undefined
d. Undefined

85. In mathematics, a _____ is the result of multiplying, or an expression that identifies factors to be multiplied.
    a. Thing
    b. Product0
    c. Undefined
    d. Undefined

86. A _____ is a set of possible values that a variable can take on in order to satisfy a given set of conditions, which may include equations and inequalities.
    a. Thing
    b. Solution set0
    c. Undefined
    d. Undefined

87. In mathematics, an _____ is a statement about the relative size or order of two objects.
    a. Thing
    b. Inequality0
    c. Undefined
    d. Undefined

88. Two mathematical objects are equal if and only if they are precisely the same in every way. This defines a binary relation, _____, denoted by the sign of _____ "=" in such a way that the statement "x = y" means that x and y are equal.
    a. Thing
    b. Equality0
    c. Undefined
    d. Undefined

89. In mathematics, _____ geometry was the traditional name for the geometry of three-dimensional Euclidean space — for practical purposes the kind of space we live in.
    a. Solid0
    b. Thing
    c. Undefined
    d. Undefined

90. In logic, and especially in its applications to mathematics and philosophy, a _____ is an exception to a proposed general rule, i.e., a specific instance of the falsity of a universal quantification (a "for all" statement).
    a. Thing
    b. Counterexample0
    c. Undefined
    d. Undefined

91. In mathematics, factorization (British English: factorisation) or factoring is the decomposition of an object (for example, a number, a polynomial, or a matrix) into a product of other objects, or _____, which when multiplied together give the original.
    a. Factors0
    b. Thing
    c. Undefined
    d. Undefined

92. _____ is a natural number that has exactly two distinct natural number divisors, which are 1 and the _____ itself.
    a. Prime number0
    b. Thing
    c. Undefined
    d. Undefined

93. In mathematics, a _____ number (or a _____) is a natural number that has exactly two (distinct) natural number divisors, which are 1 and the _____ number itself.

Chapter 5. Linear Equations and inequalities

a. Prime0
b. Thing
c. Undefined
d. Undefined

94. A _____ is the result of the addition of a set of numbers. The numbers may be natural numbers, complex numbers, matrices, or still more complicated objects. An infinite _____ is a subtle procedure known as a series.
a. Thing
b. Sum0
c. Undefined
d. Undefined

95. In mathematics, a _____ is the end result of a division problem. It can also be expressed as the number of times the divisor divides into the dividend.
a. Quotient0
b. Thing
c. Undefined
d. Undefined

96. _____ is the process of reducing the number of significant digits in a number.
a. Rounding0
b. Concept
c. Undefined
d. Undefined

97. A _____ is a one-dimensional picture in which the integers are shown as specially-marked points evenly spaced on a line.
a. Thing
b. Number line0
c. Undefined
d. Undefined

98. _____ consists of the first element in a coordinate pair. When graphed in the coordinate plane, it is the distance from the y-axis. Frequently called the x coordinate.
a. Thing
b. Abscissa0
c. Undefined
d. Undefined

99. Transport or _____ is the movement of people and goods from one place to another.
a. Transportation0
b. Thing
c. Undefined
d. Undefined

100. In geometry, the _____ of an object is a point in some sense in the middle of the object.
a. Center0
b. Thing
c. Undefined
d. Undefined

101. _____ is a form of periodic payment from an employer to an employee, which is specified in an employment contract.
a. Gross pay0
b. Thing
c. Undefined
d. Undefined

102. A _____ is a form of periodic payment from an employer to an employee, which is specified in an employment contract.
a. Thing
b. Salary0
c. Undefined
d. Undefined

Chapter 5. Linear Equations and inequalities

103. Fixed costs are expenses whose total does not change in proportion to the activity of a business.Unit fixed costs decline with volume following a retangular hyperbola as the volume of production.Variable costs by contrast change in relation to the activity of a business such as sales or production volume.Along with variable costs,fixed costs make up one of the two components of total cost. In the most simple production function total cost is equal to fixed costs plus variable costs.In accounting terminology, fixed costs will broadly include all costs which are not included in cost of goods sold, and variable costs are those captured in costs of goods sold. The implicit assumption required to make the equivalence between the accounting and economics terminology is that the accounting period is equal to the period in which fixed costs do not vary in relation to production. In practice, this equivalence does not always hold and depending on the period under consideration by management, some overhead expenses can be adjusted by management, and the specific allocation of each expense to each category will be decided under cost accounting.In business planning and management accounting, usage of the terms fixed costs, variable costs and others will often differ from usage in economics, and may depend on the intended use. For example, costs may be segregated into per unit costs fixed costs per period, and variable costs as a proportion of revenue. Capital expenditures will usually be allocated separately, and depending on the purpose, a portion may be regularly allocated to expenses as depreciation and amortization and seen as a _____ per period, or the entire amount may be considered upfront fixed costs.
- a. Fixed cost0
- b. Thing
- c. Undefined
- d. Undefined

104. _____ are expenses whose total does not change in proportion to the activity of a business, within the relevant time period or scale of production
- a. Thing
- b. Fixed costs0
- c. Undefined
- d. Undefined

105. _____ is the application of tools and a processing medium to the transformation of raw materials into finished goods for sale.
- a. Manufacturing0
- b. Thing
- c. Undefined
- d. Undefined

106. In physics, _____ is an influence that may cause an object to accelerate. It may be experienced as a lift, a push, or a pull. The actual acceleration of the body is determined by the vector sum of all forces acting on it, known as net _____ or resultant _____.
- a. Thing
- b. Force0
- c. Undefined
- d. Undefined

107. In mathematics, a _____ function in the sense of algebraic geometry is an everywhere-defined, polynomial function on an algebraic variety V with values in the field K over which V is defined.
- a. Thing
- b. Regular0
- c. Undefined
- d. Undefined

108. In chemistry, a _____ is substance made by combining two or more different materials in such a way that no chemical reaction occurs.
- a. Thing
- b. Mixture0
- c. Undefined
- d. Undefined

109. A _____ is a compensation which workers receive in exchange for their labor.

a. Wage0
c. Undefined

b. Thing
d. Undefined

Chapter 6. Systems of Linear Equations

1. The word _____ comes from the Latin word linearis, which means created by lines.
   a. Thing
   b. Linear0
   c. Undefined
   d. Undefined

2. A _____ is an equation in which each term is either a constant or the product of a constant times the first power of a variable.
   a. Thing
   b. Linear equation0
   c. Undefined
   d. Undefined

3. A _____ is a symbolic representation denoting a quantity or expression. It often represents an "unknown" quantity that has the potential to change.
   a. Thing
   b. Variable0
   c. Undefined
   d. Undefined

4. A _____ is a set of numbers that designate location in a given reference system, such as x,y in a planar _____ system or an x,y,z in a three-dimensional _____ system.
   a. Thing
   b. Coordinate0
   c. Undefined
   d. Undefined

5. An _____ is a collection of two not necessarily distinct objects, one of which is distinguished as the first coordinate and the other as the second coordinate.
   a. Ordered pair0
   b. Thing
   c. Undefined
   d. Undefined

6. A _____ is a negotiable instrument instructing a financial institution to pay a specific amount of a specific currency from a specific demand account held in the maker/depositor's name with that institution. Both the maker and payee may be natural persons or legal entities.
   a. Thing
   b. Check0
   c. Undefined
   d. Undefined

7. In mathematics, the conjugate _____ or adjoint matrix of an m-by-n matrix A with complex entries is the n-by-m matrix A* obtained from A by taking the transpose and then taking the complex conjugate of each entry.
   a. Pairs0
   b. Thing
   c. Undefined
   d. Undefined

8. _____ are the basic objects of study in graph theory. Informally speaking, a graph is a set of objects called points, nodes, or vertices connected by links called lines or edges.
   a. Graphs0
   b. Thing
   c. Undefined
   d. Undefined

9. _____ is the state of being greater than any finite real or natural number, however large.
   a. Infinite0
   b. Thing
   c. Undefined
   d. Undefined

10. The _____, the average in everyday English, which is also called the arithmetic _____ (and is distinguished from the geometric _____ or harmonic _____). The average is also called the sample _____. The expected value of a random variable, which is also called the population _____.

Chapter 6. Systems of Linear Equations

    a. Thing
    b. Mean0
    c. Undefined
    d. Undefined

11. In common philosophical language, a proposition or _____, is the content of an assertion, that is, it is true-or-false and defined by the meaning of a particular piece of language.
    a. Concept
    b. Statement0
    c. Undefined
    d. Undefined

12. In geographic information systems, a _____ comprises an entity with a geographic location, typically determined by points, arcs, or polygons. Carriageways and cadastres exemplify _____ data.
    a. Feature0
    b. Thing
    c. Undefined
    d. Undefined

13. In mathematics, the _____ of two sets A and B is the set that contains all elements of A that also belong to B (or equivalently, all elements of B that also belong to A), but no other elements.
    a. Intersection0
    b. Thing
    c. Undefined
    d. Undefined

14. The existence and properties of _____ are the basis of Euclid's parallel postulate. _____ are two lines on the same plane that do not intersect even assuming that lines extend to infinity in either direction.
    a. Thing
    b. Parallel lines0
    c. Undefined
    d. Undefined

15. In geometry, _____ lines are two lines that share one or more common points.
    a. Thing
    b. Intersecting0
    c. Undefined
    d. Undefined

16. _____ are a set of equations containing multiple variables.
    a. Systems of equations0
    b. Thing
    c. Undefined
    d. Undefined

17. _____ is a statistical measure of the average length of survival of a living thing.
    a. Thing
    b. Life expectancy0
    c. Undefined
    d. Undefined

18. The _____ is used to discard one of the variables in an equation, only to replace it with the actual value when solving multiple equations.
    a. Substitution method0
    b. Thing
    c. Undefined
    d. Undefined

19. _____ is often used to describe the measurement of the steepness, incline, gradient, or grade of a straight line. The _____ is defined as the ratio of the "rise" divided by the "run" between two points on a line, or in other words, the ratio of the altitude change to the horizontal distance between any two points on the line.
    a. Slope0
    b. Thing
    c. Undefined
    d. Undefined

Chapter 6. Systems of Linear Equations

20. In mathematics, a _____ is a constant multiplicative factor of a certain object. The object can be such things as a variable, a vector, a function, etc. For example, the _____ of $9x^2$ is 9.
    a. Thing
    b. Coefficient0
    c. Undefined
    d. Undefined

21. The _____ are the only integral domain whose positive elements are well-ordered, and in which order is preserved by addition. Like the natural numbers, the _____ form a countably infinite set. The set of all _____ is usually denoted in mathematics by a boldface Z.
    a. Integers0
    b. Thing
    c. Undefined
    d. Undefined

22. In mathematics, the additive inverse, or _____ of a number n is the number that, when added to n, yields zero. The additive inverse of n is denoted −n. For example, 7 is −7, because 7 + (−7) = 0, and the additive inverse of −0.3 is 0.3, because −0.3 + 0.3 = 0.
    a. Opposite0
    b. Thing
    c. Undefined
    d. Undefined

23. In mathematics and the mathematical sciences, a _____ is a fixed, but possibly unspecified, value. This is in contrast to a variable, which is not fixed.
    a. Thing
    b. Constant0
    c. Undefined
    d. Undefined

24. In mathematics, _____ are essentially word problems that are designed to use mathematical critical thinking in everyday situations.
    a. Thing
    b. Application problems0
    c. Undefined
    d. Undefined

25. A _____ is a special kind of ratio, indicating a relationship between two measurements with different units, such as miles to gallons or cents to pounds.
    a. Rate0
    b. Thing
    c. Undefined
    d. Undefined

26. _____ is the transport of people on a trip/journey or the process or time involved in a person or object moving from one location to another.
    a. Thing
    b. Travel0
    c. Undefined
    d. Undefined

27. In mathematics, a _____ is a two-dimensional manifold or surface that is perfectly flat.
    a. Thing
    b. Plane0
    c. Undefined
    d. Undefined

28. A _____ is the result of the addition of a set of numbers. The numbers may be natural numbers, complex numbers, matrices, or still more complicated objects. An infinite _____ is a subtle procedure known as a series.
    a. Sum0
    b. Thing
    c. Undefined
    d. Undefined

Chapter 6. Systems of Linear Equations

29. An _____ is a combination of numbers, operators, grouping symbols and/or free variables and bound variables arranged in a meaningful way which can be evaluated..
   a. Expression0
   b. Thing
   c. Undefined
   d. Undefined

30. A _____ is a craftsman who creates jewelry using jewels, precious metals, or other substances.
   a. Jeweler0
   b. Thing
   c. Undefined
   d. Undefined

31. _____ is electromagnetic radiation with a wavelength that is visible to the eye (visible _____) or, in a technical or scientific context, electromagnetic radiation of any wavelength.
   a. Thing
   b. Light0
   c. Undefined
   d. Undefined

32. In mathematics, the _____ of a number n is the number that, when added to n, yields zero. The _____ of n is denoted −n. For example, 7 is −7, because 7 + (−7) = 0, and the _____ of −0.3 is 0.3, because −0.3 + 0.3 = 0.
   a. Thing
   b. Additive inverse0
   c. Undefined
   d. Undefined

33. _____ is a kind of property which exists as magnitude or multitude. It is among the basic classes of things along with quality, substance, change, and relation.
   a. Amount0
   b. Thing
   c. Undefined
   d. Undefined

34. In finance and economics, _____ is the process of finding the present value of an amount of cash at some future date, and along with compounding cash forms the basis of time value of money calculations.
   a. Thing
   b. Discount0
   c. Undefined
   d. Undefined

35. A _____ is a fee added to a customer's bill.
   a. Thing
   b. Service charge0
   c. Undefined
   d. Undefined

36. In mathematics, a _____ function in the sense of algebraic geometry is an everywhere-defined, polynomial function on an algebraic variety V with values in the field K over which V is defined.
   a. Regular0
   b. Thing
   c. Undefined
   d. Undefined

37. In Graph theory, a _____ is a digraph with weighted edges.
   a. Concept
   b. Network0
   c. Undefined
   d. Undefined

38. In mathematics, a _____ number (or a _____) is a natural number that has exactly two (distinct) natural number divisors, which are 1 and the _____ number itself.

Chapter 6. Systems of Linear Equations

   a. Thing
   c. Undefined
   b. Prime0
   d. Undefined

39. _____ are activities that are governed by a set of rules or customs and often engaged in competitively.
   a. Sports0
   c. Undefined
   b. Thing
   d. Undefined

40. _____ is the general term that is used to describe physical artifacts of a technology.
   a. Hardware0
   c. Undefined
   b. Thing
   d. Undefined

41. A pair of angles is _____ if their respective measures sum to 180 degrees.
   a. Concept
   c. Undefined
   b. Supplementary0
   d. Undefined

42. A _____ is a function that assigns a number to subsets of a given set.
   a. Thing
   c. Undefined
   b. Measure0
   d. Undefined

43. A _____ is the part of the dividend that is left over when the dividend is not evenly divisible by the divisor.
   a. Thing
   c. Undefined
   b. Remainder0
   d. Undefined

44. _____ is the fee paid on borrowed money.
   a. Thing
   c. Undefined
   b. Interest0
   d. Undefined

45. _____ or investing is a term with several closely-related meanings in business management, finance and economics, related to saving or deferring consumption.
   a. Thing
   c. Undefined
   b. Investment0
   d. Undefined

46. _____ forms part of thinking. Considered the most complex of all intellectual functions, _____ has been defined as higher-order cognitive process that requires the modulation and control of more routine or fundamental skills.
   a. Thing
   c. Undefined
   b. Problem solving0
   d. Undefined

47. A _____ fraction is a fraction in which the absolute value of the numerator is less than the denominator--hence, the absolute value of the fraction is less than 1.
   a. Thing
   c. Undefined
   b. Proper0
   d. Undefined

48. In mathematics, factorization (British English: factorisation) or factoring is the decomposition of an object (for example, a number, a polynomial, or a matrix) into a product of other objects, or _____, which when multiplied together give the original.

Chapter 6. Systems of Linear Equations

    a. Thing   b. Factors0
    c. Undefined   d. Undefined

49. A _____ is defined as an integer which is the sum of the positive divisors not including the number.
    a. Perfect number0   b. Thing
    c. Undefined   d. Undefined

50. In mathematics, a _____ of an integer n, also called a factor of n, is an integer which evenly divides n without leaving a remainder.
    a. Divisor0   b. Thing
    c. Undefined   d. Undefined

51. In mathematics, a _____ can mean either an element of the set {1, 2, 3, ...} (i.e the positive integers or the counting numbers) or an element of the set {0, 1, 2, 3, ...} (i.e. the non-negative integers).
    a. Natural number0   b. Thing
    c. Undefined   d. Undefined

52. _____ is a natural number that has exactly two distinct natural number divisors, which are 1 and the _____ itself.
    a. Thing   b. Prime number0
    c. Undefined   d. Undefined

53. In mathematics, an inequality is a statement about the relative size or order of two objects. For example 14 > 10, or 14 is _____ 10.
    a. Thing   b. Greater than0
    c. Undefined   d. Undefined

54. In mathematics, _____ is the decomposition of an object into a product of other objects, or factors, which when multiplied together give the original.
    a. Factoring0   b. Thing
    c. Undefined   d. Undefined

55. _____, in number theory is the process of breaking down a composite number into smaller non-trivial divisors, which when multiplied together equal the original integer.
    a. Integer factorization0   b. Thing
    c. Undefined   d. Undefined

56. In mathematics, a matrix can be thought of as each row or _____ being a vector. Hence, a space formed by row vectors or _____ vectors are said to be a row space or a _____ space.
    a. Column0   b. Concept
    c. Undefined   d. Undefined

57. In mathematics, _____ growth occurs when the growth rate of a function is always proportional to the function's current size.

Chapter 6. Systems of Linear Equations

a. Thing
c. Undefined
b. Exponential0
d. Undefined

58. In mathematics, a _____ is the result of multiplying, or an expression that identifies factors to be multiplied.
a. Thing
c. Undefined
b. Product0
d. Undefined

59. The _____ of measurement are a globally standardized and modernized form of the metric system.
a. Units0
c. Undefined
b. Thing
d. Undefined

60. _____ is a business term for the amount of money that a company receives from its activities in a given period, mostly from sales of products and/or services to customers
a. Revenue0
c. Undefined
b. Thing
d. Undefined

61. Fixed costs are expenses whose total does not change in proportion to the activity of a business.Unit fixed costs decline with volume following a retangular hyperbola as the volume of production.Variable costs by contrast change in relation to the activity of a business such as sales or production volume.Along with variable costs,fixed costs make up one of the two components of total cost. In the most simple production function total cost is equal to fixed costs plus variable costs.In accounting terminology, fixed costs will broadly include all costs which are not included in cost of goods sold, and variable costs are those captured in costs of goods sold. The implicit assumption required to make the equivalence between the accounting and economics terminology is that the accounting period is equal to the period in which fixed costs do not vary in relation to production. In practice, this equivalence does not always hold and depending on the period under consideration by management, some overhead expenses can be adjusted by management, and the specific allocation of each expense to each category will be decided under cost accounting.In business planning and management accounting, usage of the terms fixed costs, variable costs and others will often differ from usage in economics, and may depend on the intended use. For example, costs may be segregated into per unit costs fixed costs per period, and variable costs as a proportion of revenue. Capital expenditures will usually be allocated separately, and depending on the purpose, a portion may be regularly allocated to expenses as depreciation and amortization and seen as a _____ per period, or the entire amount may be considered upfront fixed costs.
a. Thing
c. Undefined
b. Fixed cost0
d. Undefined

62. _____ are expenses whose total does not change in proportion to the activity of a business, within the relevant time period or scale of production
a. Fixed costs0
c. Undefined
b. Thing
d. Undefined

63. A _____ consists of one quarter of the coordinate plane.
a. Quadrant0
c. Undefined
b. Thing
d. Undefined

64. An _____ is a straight line around which a geometric figure can be rotated.

Chapter 6. Systems of Linear Equations

a. Thing
b. Axis0
c. Undefined
d. Undefined

65. The _____ is the y- coordinate of a point within a two dimensional coordinate system. It is sometimes used to refer to the axis rather than the distance along the coordinate system.
a. Thing
b. Ordinate0
c. Undefined
d. Undefined

66. In astronomy, geography, geometry and related sciences and contexts, a plane is said to be _____ at a given point if it is locally perpendicular to the gradient of the gravity field, i.e., with the direction of the gravitational force at that point.
a. Horizontal0
b. Thing
c. Undefined
d. Undefined

67. _____ is the application of tools and a processing medium to the transformation of raw materials into finished goods for sale.
a. Manufacturing0
b. Thing
c. Undefined
d. Undefined

68. In mathematics and its applications, a _____ is a system for assigning an n-tuple of numbers or scalars to each point in an n-dimensional space.
a. Coordinate system0
b. Concept
c. Undefined
d. Undefined

69. In mathematics, _____ is an elementary arithmetic operation. When one of the numbers is a whole number, _____ is the repeated sum of the other number.
a. Thing
b. Multiplication0
c. Undefined
d. Undefined

70. Multiple Signal Classification, also known as _____, is an algorithm used for frequency estimation and emitter location.
a. Thing
b. Music0
c. Undefined
d. Undefined

71. In mathematics, a subset of Euclidean space R^n is called _____ if it is closed and bounded.
a. Thing
b. Compact0
c. Undefined
d. Undefined

72. In chemistry, a _____ is substance made by combining two or more different materials in such a way that no chemical reaction occurs.
a. Thing
b. Mixture0
c. Undefined
d. Undefined

73. In mathematics, the _____ of a function is the set of all "output" values produced by that function. Given a function $f : A \to B$, the _____ of f, is defined to be the set $\{x \in B : x = f(a) \text{ for some } a \in A\}$.

Chapter 6. Systems of Linear Equations

a. Range0
b. Thing
c. Undefined
d. Undefined

74. A _____ is a set of possible values that a variable can take on in order to satisfy a given set of conditions, which may include equations and inequalities.
    a. Solution set0
    b. Thing
    c. Undefined
    d. Undefined

75. In mathematics, a _____ of a k-place relation $L \subseteq X_1 \times ... \times X_k$ is one of the sets X_j, $1 \leq j \leq k$. In the special case where k = 2 and $L \subseteq X_1 \times X_2$ is a function $L : X_1 \to X_2$, it is conventional to refer to X_1 as the _____ of the function and to refer to X_2 as the codomain of the function.
    a. Thing
    b. Domain0
    c. Undefined
    d. Undefined

76. The mathematical concept of a _____ expresses the intuitive idea of deterministic dependence between two quantities, one of which is viewed as primary and the other as secondary. A _____ then is a way to associate a unique output for each input of a specified type, for example, a real number or an element of a given set.
    a. Function0
    b. Thing
    c. Undefined
    d. Undefined

77. The _____ of a ring R is defined to be the smallest positive integer n such that $n\,a = 0$, for all a in R.
    a. Characteristic0
    b. Thing
    c. Undefined
    d. Undefined

78. In sociology and biology a _____ is the collection of people or organisms of a particular species living in a given geographic area or space, usually measured by a census.
    a. Thing
    b. Population0
    c. Undefined
    d. Undefined

79. _____ is mass m per unit volume V.
    a. Thing
    b. Density0
    c. Undefined
    d. Undefined

80. In mathematical analysis, _____ are objects which generalize functions and probability distributions.
    a. Thing
    b. Distribution0
    c. Undefined
    d. Undefined

81. _____ is the scientific study of celestial objects such as stars, planets, comets, and galaxies; and phenomena that originate outside the Earth's atmosphere.
    a. Astronomy0
    b. Thing
    c. Undefined
    d. Undefined

82. Compass and straightedge or ruler-and-compass _____ is the _____ of lengths or angles using only an idealized ruler and compass.

Chapter 6. Systems of Linear Equations

a. Construction0
b. Thing
c. Undefined
d. Undefined

83. _____ is a term used in marketing to indicate how much the price of a product is above the cost of producing and distributing the product.

a. Thing
b. Markup0
c. Undefined
d. Undefined

84. _____, Greek for "knowledge of nature," is the branch of science concerned with the discovery and characterization of universal laws which govern matter, energy, space, and time.

a. Thing
b. Physics0
c. Undefined
d. Undefined

Chapter 7. Polynomials

1. In mathematics, a _____ is a particular kind of polynomial, having just one term.
   - a. Thing
   - b. Monomial0
   - c. Undefined
   - d. Undefined

2. In mathematics, a _____ is the result of multiplying, or an expression that identifies factors to be multiplied.
   - a. Product0
   - b. Thing
   - c. Undefined
   - d. Undefined

3. A _____ is a symbolic representation denoting a quantity or expression. It often represents an "unknown" quantity that has the potential to change.
   - a. Thing
   - b. Variable0
   - c. Undefined
   - d. Undefined

4. In mathematics, a _____ is an expression that is constructed from one or more variables and constants, using only the operations of addition, subtraction, multiplication, and constant positive whole number exponents. is a _____. Note in particular that division by an expression containing a variable is not in general allowed in polynomials. [1]
   - a. Thing
   - b. Polynomial0
   - c. Undefined
   - d. Undefined

5. In mathematics, a _____ is the end result of a division problem. It can also be expressed as the number of times the divisor divides into the dividend.
   - a. Thing
   - b. Quotient0
   - c. Undefined
   - d. Undefined

6. An _____ is a combination of numbers, operators, grouping symbols and/or free variables and bound variables arranged in a meaningful way which can be evaluated..
   - a. Thing
   - b. Expression0
   - c. Undefined
   - d. Undefined

7. _____ is a mathematical operation, written a^n, involving two numbers, the base a and the exponent n.
   - a. Exponentiating0
   - b. Thing
   - c. Undefined
   - d. Undefined

8. _____ is a mathematical operation, written a^n, involving two numbers, the base a and the exponent n.
   - a. Thing
   - b. Exponentiation0
   - c. Undefined
   - d. Undefined

9. In mathematics, there are several meanings of _____ depending on the subject.
   - a. Degree0
   - b. Thing
   - c. Undefined
   - d. Undefined

10. The _____ is the maximum of the degrees of all terms in the polynomial.
    - a. Degree of a polynomial0
    - b. Thing
    - c. Undefined
    - d. Undefined

11. In mathematics and the mathematical sciences, a _____ is a fixed, but possibly unspecified, value. This is in contrast to a variable, which is not fixed.

Chapter 7. Polynomials

a. Thing
b. Constant0
c. Undefined
d. Undefined

12. In astronomy, geography, geometry and related sciences and contexts, a plane is said to be _____ at a given point if it is locally perpendicular to the gradient of the gravity field, i.e., with the direction of the gravitational force at that point.
    a. Horizontal0
    b. Thing
    c. Undefined
    d. Undefined

13. In mathematics, a matrix can be thought of as each row or _____ being a vector. Hence, a space formed by row vectors or _____ vectors are said to be a row space or a _____ space.
    a. Column0
    b. Concept
    c. Undefined
    d. Undefined

14. In mathematics, the additive inverse, or _____ of a number n is the number that, when added to n, yields zero. The additive inverse of n is denoted −n. For example, 7 is −7, because 7 + (−7) = 0, and the additive inverse of −0.3 is 0.3, because −0.3 + 0.3 = 0.
    a. Thing
    b. Opposite0
    c. Undefined
    d. Undefined

15. _____, either of the curved-bracket punctuation marks that together make a set of _____
    a. Thing
    b. Parentheses0
    c. Undefined
    d. Undefined

16. In mathematics, the _____ of a number n is the number that, when added to n, yields zero. The _____ of n is denoted −n. For example, 7 is −7, because 7 + (−7) = 0, and the _____ of −0.3 is 0.3, because −0.3 + 0.3 = 0.
    a. Thing
    b. Additive inverse0
    c. Undefined
    d. Undefined

17. In mathematics, a _____ is a constant multiplicative factor of a certain object. The object can be such things as a variable, a vector, a function, etc. For example, the _____ of $9x^2$ is 9.
    a. Coefficient0
    b. Thing
    c. Undefined
    d. Undefined

18. A _____ is a polynomial consisting of three terms; in other words, it is the sum of three monomials.
    a. Thing
    b. Trinomial0
    c. Undefined
    d. Undefined

19. In elementary algebra, a _____ is a polynomial with two terms: the sum of two monomials. It is the simplest kind of polynomial except for a monomial.
    a. Binomial0
    b. Thing
    c. Undefined
    d. Undefined

20. In mathematics, _____ is an elementary arithmetic operation. When one of the numbers is a whole number, _____ is the repeated sum of the other number.

a. Multiplication0
b. Thing
c. Undefined
d. Undefined

21. In mathematics, _____ growth occurs when the growth rate of a function is always proportional to the function's current size.
    a. Thing
    b. Exponential0
    c. Undefined
    d. Undefined

22. In mathematics, factorization (British English: factorisation) or factoring is the decomposition of an object (for example, a number, a polynomial, or a matrix) into a product of other objects, or _____, which when multiplied together give the original.
    a. Thing
    b. Factors0
    c. Undefined
    d. Undefined

23. The _____ are the only integral domain whose positive elements are well-ordered, and in which order is preserved by addition. Like the natural numbers, the _____ form a countably infinite set. The set of all _____ is usually denoted in mathematics by a boldface Z .
    a. Integers0
    b. Thing
    c. Undefined
    d. Undefined

24. A _____ is a three-dimensional solid object bounded by six square faces, facets, or sides, with three meeting at each vertex.
    a. Cube0
    b. Thing
    c. Undefined
    d. Undefined

25. _____ has many meanings, most of which simply .
    a. Power0
    b. Thing
    c. Undefined
    d. Undefined

26. In mathematics, _____ expressions is used to reduce the expression into the lowest possible term.
    a. Thing
    b. Simplifying0
    c. Undefined
    d. Undefined

27. In common philosophical language, a proposition or _____, is the content of an assertion, that is, it is true-or-false and defined by the meaning of a particular piece of language.
    a. Statement0
    b. Concept
    c. Undefined
    d. Undefined

28. The _____, the average in everyday English, which is also called the arithmetic _____ (and is distinguished from the geometric _____ or harmonic _____). The average is also called the sample _____. The expected value of a random variable, which is also called the population _____.
    a. Mean0
    b. Thing
    c. Undefined
    d. Undefined

29. In mathematics, and in particular in abstract algebra, the _____ is a property of binary operations that generalises the distributive law from elementary algebra.

Chapter 7. Polynomials

    a. Thing
    b. Distributive property0
    c. Undefined
    d. Undefined

30. In mathematics, a _____ can mean either an element of the set {1, 2, 3, ...} (i.e the positive integers) or an element of the set {0, 1, 2, 3, ...} (i.e. the non-negative integers).
    a. Concept
    b. Whole number0
    c. Undefined
    d. Undefined

31. A _____ is the result of the addition of a set of numbers. The numbers may be natural numbers, complex numbers, matrices, or still more complicated objects. An infinite _____ is a subtle procedure known as a series.
    a. Sum0
    b. Thing
    c. Undefined
    d. Undefined

32. In plane geometry, a _____ is a polygon with four equal sides, four right angles, and parallel opposite sides. In algebra, the _____ of a number is that number multiplied by itself.
    a. Thing
    b. Square0
    c. Undefined
    d. Undefined

33. In Euclidean geometry, a _____ is the set of all points in a plane at a fixed distance, called the radius, from a given point, the center.
    a. Circle0
    b. Thing
    c. Undefined
    d. Undefined

34. In classical geometry, a _____ of a circle or sphere is any line segment from its center to its boundary. By extension, the _____ of a circle or sphere is the length of any such segment. The _____ is half the diameter. In science and engineering the term _____ of curvature is commonly used as a synonym for _____.
    a. Thing
    b. Radius0
    c. Undefined
    d. Undefined

35. In mathematics, _____ are essentially word problems that are designed to use mathematical critical thinking in everyday situations.
    a. Thing
    b. Application problems0
    c. Undefined
    d. Undefined

36. In geometry, a _____ is defined as a quadrilateral where all four of its angles are right angles.
    a. Thing
    b. Rectangle0
    c. Undefined
    d. Undefined

37. A _____ is one of the basic shapes of geometry: a polygon with three vertices and three sides which are straight line segments.
    a. Thing
    b. Triangle0
    c. Undefined
    d. Undefined

38. _____ also sometimes known as the double distributive property or more colloquially as foiling, is commonly taught to US high school students learning algebra as a mnemonic for remembering how to multiply two binomials polynomials with two terms.

Chapter 7. Polynomials

a. Thing
b. FOIL method0
c. Undefined
d. Undefined

39. The _____ is commonly taught to US high school students learning algebra as a mnemonic for remembering how to multiply two binomials.
   a. FOIL rule0
   b. Thing
   c. Undefined
   d. Undefined

40. _____ are activities that are governed by a set of rules or customs and often engaged in competitively.
   a. Thing
   b. Sports0
   c. Undefined
   d. Undefined

41. A _____ is a numeral used to indicate a count. The most common use of the word today is to name the part of a fraction that tells the number or count of equal parts.
   a. Numerator0
   b. Thing
   c. Undefined
   d. Undefined

42. A _____ is the part of a fraction that tells how many equal parts make up a whole, and which is used in the name of the fraction: "halves", "thirds", "fourths" or "quarters", "fifths" and so on.
   a. Concept
   b. Denominator0
   c. Undefined
   d. Undefined

43. _____ is the largest positive integer that divides both numbers without remainder.
   a. Common Factor0
   b. Thing
   c. Undefined
   d. Undefined

44. Sir Isaac _____, was an English physicist, mathematician, astronomer, natural philosopher, and alchemist, regarded by many as the greatest figure in the history of science
   a. Person
   b. Newton0
   c. Undefined
   d. Undefined

45. Mathematical _____ is used to represent ideas.
   a. Notation0
   b. Thing
   c. Undefined
   d. Undefined

46. _____ is the writing of numbers in the base-ten numeral system, which uses various symbols called digits for ten distinct values 0, 1, 2, 3, 4, 5, 6, 7, 8 and 9 to represent numbers
   a. Thing
   b. Decimal notation0
   c. Undefined
   d. Undefined

47. _____ is a notation for writing numbers that is often used by scientists and mathematicians to make it easier to write large and small numbers.
   a. Scientific notation0
   b. Thing
   c. Undefined
   d. Undefined

Chapter 7. Polynomials

48. The decimal separator is a symbol used to mark the boundary between the integral and the fractional parts of a decimal numeral. Terms implying the symbol used are _____ and decimal comma.
    a. Decimal point0
    b. Concept
    c. Undefined
    d. Undefined

49. In mathematics, the _____ (or modulus) of a real number is its numerical value without regard to its sign.
    a. Absolute value0
    b. Thing
    c. Undefined
    d. Undefined

50. A _____ is a number that is less than zero.
    a. Negative number0
    b. Thing
    c. Undefined
    d. Undefined

51. In mathematics, the multiplicative inverse of a number x, denoted 1/x or x^{-1}, is the number which, when multiplied by x, yields 1. The multiplicative inverse of x is also called the _____ of x.
    a. Reciprocal0
    b. Thing
    c. Undefined
    d. Undefined

52. _____ is the transport of people on a trip/journey or the process or time involved in a person or object moving from one location to another.
    a. Thing
    b. Travel0
    c. Undefined
    d. Undefined

53. _____ is electromagnetic radiation with a wavelength that is visible to the eye (visible _____) or, in a technical or scientific context, electromagnetic radiation of any wavelength.
    a. Thing
    b. Light0
    c. Undefined
    d. Undefined

54. _____ is the property of a physical object that quantifies the amount of matter and energy it is equivalent to.
    a. Mass0
    b. Thing
    c. Undefined
    d. Undefined

55. _____ is the estimation of a physical quantity such as distance, energy, temperature, or time.
    a. Measurement0
    b. Thing
    c. Undefined
    d. Undefined

56. The _____ or parallactic second is a unit of length used in astronomy.
    a. Thing
    b. Parsec0
    c. Undefined
    d. Undefined

57. A _____ is a function that assigns a number to subsets of a given set.
    a. Thing
    b. Measure0
    c. Undefined
    d. Undefined

58. _____ is the scientific study of celestial objects such as stars, planets, comets, and galaxies; and phenomena that originate outside the Earth's atmosphere.

Chapter 7. Polynomials

a. Astronomy0
b. Thing
c. Undefined
d. Undefined

59. A _____ is a negotiable instrument instructing a financial institution to pay a specific amount of a specific currency from a specific demand account held in the maker/depositor's name with that institution. Both the maker and payee may be natural persons or legal entities.
a. Check0
b. Thing
c. Undefined
d. Undefined

60. A _____ is the part of the dividend that is left over when the dividend is not evenly divisible by the divisor.
a. Thing
b. Remainder0
c. Undefined
d. Undefined

61. _____ is a payment made by a company to its shareholders
a. Dividend0
b. Thing
c. Undefined
d. Undefined

62. In mathematics, a _____ of an integer n, also called a factor of n, is an integer which evenly divides n without leaving a remainder.
a. Thing
b. Divisor0
c. Undefined
d. Undefined

63. A _____ fraction is a fraction in which the absolute value of the numerator is less than the denominator--hence, the absolute value of the fraction is less than 1.
a. Thing
b. Proper0
c. Undefined
d. Undefined

64. The _____ of measurement are a globally standardized and modernized form of the metric system.
a. Units0
b. Thing
c. Undefined
d. Undefined

65. _____ is a conceptual tool often applied in physics, chemistry, and engineering to understand physical situations involving a mix of different kinds of physical quantities.
a. Dimensional analysis0
b. Concept
c. Undefined
d. Undefined

66. A _____ is a deliberate process for transforming one or more inputs into one or more results.
a. Calculation0
b. Thing
c. Undefined
d. Undefined

67. The metre (or _____, see spelling differences) is a measure of length. It is the basic unit of length in the metric system and in the International System of Units (SI), used around the world for general and scientific purposes.
a. Meter0
b. Concept
c. Undefined
d. Undefined

Chapter 7. Polynomials

68. The _____ of a solid object is the three-dimensional concept of how much space it occupies, often quantified numerically.
   a. Thing
   b. Volume0
   c. Undefined
   d. Undefined

69. _____ is a concept in traditional logic referring to a "type of immediate inference in which from a given proposition another proposition is inferred which has as its subject the predicate of the original proposition and as its predicate the subject of the original proposition (the quality of the proposition being retained)."
   a. Concept
   b. Conversion0
   c. Undefined
   d. Undefined

70. In mathematics, an _____, mean, or central tendency of a data set refers to a measure of the "middle" or "expected" value of the data set.
   a. Average0
   b. Concept
   c. Undefined
   d. Undefined

71. A _____ is a unit of length in the metric system, equal to one thousand metres, the current SI base unit of length
   a. Kilometer0
   b. Thing
   c. Undefined
   d. Undefined

72. U.S. liquid _____ is legally defined as 231 cubic inches, and is equal to 3.785411784 litres or abotu 0.13368 cubic feet. This is the most common definition of a _____. The U.S. fluid ounce is defined as 1/128 of a U.S. _____.
   a. Thing
   b. Gallon0
   c. Undefined
   d. Undefined

73. A _____ is a unit of length, usually used to measure distance, in a number of different systems, including Imperial units, United States customary units and Norwegian/Swedish mil. Its size can vary from system to system, but in each is between 1 and 10 kilometers. In contemporary English contexts _____ refers to either:
   a. Mile0
   b. Thing
   c. Undefined
   d. Undefined

74. _____ is a unit of speed, expressing the number of international miles covered per hour.
   a. Thing
   b. Miles per hour0
   c. Undefined
   d. Undefined

75. Blaise _____ was a French mathematician, physicist, and religious philosopher.
   a. Person
   b. Pascal0
   c. Undefined
   d. Undefined

76. An _____ of a product of sums expresses it as a sum of products by using the fact that multiplication distributes over addition.
   a. Thing
   b. Expansion0
   c. Undefined
   d. Undefined

77. The _____ is the total number of human beings alive on the planet Earth at a given time.

a. World population0   b. Thing
c. Undefined   d. Undefined

78. In sociology and biology a _____ is the collection of people or organisms of a particular species living in a given geographic area or space, usually measured by a census.
    a. Population0   b. Thing
    c. Undefined   d. Undefined

79. In statistics, a _____ measure is one which is measuring what is supposed to measure.
    a. Valid0   b. Thing
    c. Undefined   d. Undefined

80. _____ are the basic objects of study in graph theory. Informally speaking, a graph is a set of objects called points, nodes, or vertices connected by links called lines or edges.
    a. Graphs0   b. Thing
    c. Undefined   d. Undefined

81. In mathematics, a _____ is a mathematical statement which appears likely to be true, but has not been formally proven to be true under the rules of mathematical logic.
    a. Concept   b. Conjecture0
    c. Undefined   d. Undefined

82. Acid _____ ratio measures the ability of a company to use its near cash or quick assets to immediately extinguish its current liabilities.
    a. Thing   b. Test0
    c. Undefined   d. Undefined

83. In mathematics, an inequality is a statement about the relative size or order of two objects. For example 14 > 10, or 14 is _____ 10.
    a. Thing   b. Greater than0
    c. Undefined   d. Undefined

84. A _____ is a set of numbers that designate location in a given reference system, such as x,y in a planar _____ system or an x,y,z in a three-dimensional _____ system.
    a. Coordinate0   b. Thing
    c. Undefined   d. Undefined

85. _____ is often used to describe the measurement of the steepness, incline, gradient, or grade of a straight line. The _____ is defined as the ratio of the "rise" divided by the "run" between two points on a line, or in other words, the ratio of the altitude change to the horizontal distance between any two points on the line.
    a. Thing   b. Slope0
    c. Undefined   d. Undefined

86. _____ element of an element x with respect to a binary operation * with identity element e is an element y such that x * y = y * x = e. In particular,

Chapter 7. Polynomials

a. Inverse0
b. Thing
c. Undefined
d. Undefined

87. In mathematics, the _____ of a function is the set of all "output" values produced by that function. Given a function $f : A \rightarrow B$, the _____ of f, is defined to be the set $\{x \in B : x = f(a) \text{ for some } a \in A\}$.

a. Thing
b. Range0
c. Undefined
d. Undefined

88. The mathematical concept of a _____ expresses the intuitive idea of deterministic dependence between two quantities, one of which is viewed as primary and the other as secondary. A _____ then is a way to associate a unique output for each input of a specified type, for example, a real number or an element of a given set.

a. Thing
b. Function0
c. Undefined
d. Undefined

89. In mathematics, a _____ of a k-place relation $L \subseteq X_1 \times \ldots \times X_k$ is one of the sets X_j, $1 \leq j \leq k$. In the special case where k = 2 and $L \subseteq X_1 \times X_2$ is a function $L : X_1 \rightarrow X_2$, it is conventional to refer to X_1 as the _____ of the function and to refer to X_2 as the codomain of the function.

a. Thing
b. Domain0
c. Undefined
d. Undefined

90. A _____ is a special kind of ratio, indicating a relationship between two measurements with different units, such as miles to gallons or cents to pounds.

a. Rate0
b. Thing
c. Undefined
d. Undefined

91. _____ is a term used in marketing to indicate how much the price of a product is above the cost of producing and distributing the product.

a. Thing
b. Markup0
c. Undefined
d. Undefined

92. In finance and economics, _____ is the process of finding the present value of an amount of cash at some future date, and along with compounding cash forms the basis of time value of money calculations.

a. Discount0
b. Thing
c. Undefined
d. Undefined

93. _____ or investing is a term with several closely-related meanings in business management, finance and economics, related to saving or deferring consumption.

a. Thing
b. Investment0
c. Undefined
d. Undefined

94. _____ is a natural number that has exactly two distinct natural number divisors, which are 1 and the _____ itself.

a. Prime number0
b. Thing
c. Undefined
d. Undefined

Chapter 7. Polynomials

95. In mathematics, a _____ number (or a _____) is a natural number that has exactly two (distinct) natural number divisors, which are 1 and the _____ number itself.
   a. Prime0
   b. Thing
   c. Undefined
   d. Undefined

96. _____ means "constancy", i.e. if something retains a certain feature even after we change a way of looking at it, then it is symmetric.
   a. Symmetry0
   b. Thing
   c. Undefined
   d. Undefined

97. _____ is a physical property of a system that underlies the common notions of hot and cold; something that is hotter has the greater _____.
   a. Temperature0
   b. Thing
   c. Undefined
   d. Undefined

98. In mathematics, a _____ is a two-dimensional manifold or surface that is perfectly flat.
   a. Plane0
   b. Thing
   c. Undefined
   d. Undefined

99. In mathematics, _____ are two-dimensional manifolds or surfaces that are perfectly flat.
   a. Planes0
   b. Thing
   c. Undefined
   d. Undefined

100. _____ of an object is its speed in a particular direction.
   a. Thing
   b. Velocity0
   c. Undefined
   d. Undefined

101. _____ are a measure of time.
   a. Minutes0
   b. Thing
   c. Undefined
   d. Undefined

102. Initial objects are also called _____, and terminal objects are also called final.
   a. Thing
   b. Coterminal0
   c. Undefined
   d. Undefined

103. In geometry, an _____ of a triangle is a straight line through a vertex and perpendicular to (i.e. forming a right angle with) the opposite side or an extension of the opposite side.
   a. Concept
   b. Altitude0
   c. Undefined
   d. Undefined

Chapter 8. Factoring

1. In mathematics, a _____ is a particular kind of polynomial, having just one term.
   a. Thing
   b. Monomial0
   c. Undefined
   d. Undefined

2. In mathematics, the _____ divisor of two non-zero integers, is the largest positive integer that divides both numbers without remainder.
   a. Thing
   b. Greatest common0
   c. Undefined
   d. Undefined

3. In Math the greates common divisor sometimes known as the _____ of two non- zero integers.
   a. Thing
   b. Greatest common factor0
   c. Undefined
   d. Undefined

4. _____ is the largest positive integer that divides both numbers without remainder.
   a. Thing
   b. Common Factor0
   c. Undefined
   d. Undefined

5. In mathematics, factorization (British English: factorisation) or factoring is the decomposition of an object (for example, a number, a polynomial, or a matrix) into a product of other objects, or _____, which when multiplied together give the original.
   a. Factors0
   b. Thing
   c. Undefined
   d. Undefined

6. The _____ are the only integral domain whose positive elements are well-ordered, and in which order is preserved by addition. Like the natural numbers, the _____ form a countably infinite set. The set of all _____ is usually denoted in mathematics by a boldface Z .
   a. Thing
   b. Integers0
   c. Undefined
   d. Undefined

7. In mathematics, a _____ is the result of multiplying, or an expression that identifies factors to be multiplied.
   a. Product0
   b. Thing
   c. Undefined
   d. Undefined

8. A _____ is a symbolic representation denoting a quantity or expression. It often represents an "unknown" quantity that has the potential to change.
   a. Variable0
   b. Thing
   c. Undefined
   d. Undefined

9. In mathematics, a _____ is an expression that is constructed from one or more variables and constants, using only the operations of addition, subtraction, multiplication, and constant positive whole number exponents. is a _____. Note in particular that division by an expression containing a variable is not in general allowed in polynomials. [1]
   a. Thing
   b. Polynomial0
   c. Undefined
   d. Undefined

10. In mathematics, and in particular in abstract algebra, the _____ is a property of binary operations that generalises the distributive law from elementary algebra.

a. Distributive property0
b. Thing
c. Undefined
d. Undefined

11. The _____, the average in everyday English, which is also called the arithmetic _____ (and is distinguished from the geometric _____ or harmonic _____). The average is also called the sample _____. The expected value of a random variable, which is also called the population _____.
   a. Mean0
   b. Thing
   c. Undefined
   d. Undefined

12. In mathematics, a _____ is the end result of a division problem. It can also be expressed as the number of times the divisor divides into the dividend.
   a. Quotient0
   b. Thing
   c. Undefined
   d. Undefined

13. An _____ is a combination of numbers, operators, grouping symbols and/or free variables and bound variables arranged in a meaningful way which can be evaluated..
   a. Expression0
   b. Thing
   c. Undefined
   d. Undefined

14. In elementary algebra, a _____ is a polynomial with two terms: the sum of two monomials. It is the simplest kind of polynomial except for a monomial.
   a. Binomial0
   b. Thing
   c. Undefined
   d. Undefined

15. In abstract algebra, _____ consists of sets with binary operations that satisfy certain axioms.
   a. Grouping0
   b. Thing
   c. Undefined
   d. Undefined

16. In common philosophical language, a proposition or _____, is the content of an assertion, that is, it is true-or-false and defined by the meaning of a particular piece of language.
   a. Statement0
   b. Concept
   c. Undefined
   d. Undefined

17. In mathematics, _____ is an elementary arithmetic operation. When one of the numbers is a whole number, _____ is the repeated sum of the other number.
   a. Multiplication0
   b. Thing
   c. Undefined
   d. Undefined

18. A _____ is the result of the addition of a set of numbers. The numbers may be natural numbers, complex numbers, matrices, or still more complicated objects. An infinite _____ is a subtle procedure known as a series.
   a. Sum0
   b. Thing
   c. Undefined
   d. Undefined

19. In mathematics, a _____ can mean either an element of the set {1, 2, 3, ...} (i.e the positive integers) or an element of the set {0, 1, 2, 3, ...} (i.e. the non-negative integers).

Chapter 8. Factoring

a. Whole number0
c. Undefined
b. Concept
d. Undefined

20. A _____ is defined as an integer which is the sum of the positive divisors not including the number.
a. Perfect number0
b. Thing
c. Undefined
d. Undefined

21. A _____ is a polynomial consisting of three terms; in other words, it is the sum of three monomials.
a. Trinomial0
b. Thing
c. Undefined
d. Undefined

22. In mathematics, a _____ is a constant multiplicative factor of a certain object. The object can be such things as a variable, a vector, a function, etc. For example, the _____ of $9x^2$ is 9.
a. Coefficient0
b. Thing
c. Undefined
d. Undefined

23. In mathematics, the additive inverse, or _____ of a number n is the number that, when added to n, yields zero. The additive inverse of n is denoted −n. For example, 7 is −7, because 7 + (−7) = 0, and the additive inverse of −0.3 is 0.3, because −0.3 + 0.3 = 0.
a. Opposite0
b. Thing
c. Undefined
d. Undefined

24. In mathematics, _____ is the decomposition of an object into a product of other objects, or factors, which when multiplied together give the original.
a. Thing
b. Factoring0
c. Undefined
d. Undefined

25. In mathematics and the mathematical sciences, a _____ is a fixed, but possibly unspecified, value. This is in contrast to a variable, which is not fixed.
a. Constant0
b. Thing
c. Undefined
d. Undefined

26. _____ is a fixed, but possibly unspecified, value. This is in contrast to a variable, which is not fixed.
a. Thing
b. Constant term0
c. Undefined
d. Undefined

27. In mathematics, the _____ of a number n is the number that, when added to n, yields zero. The _____ of n is denoted −n. For example, 7 is −7, because 7 + (−7) = 0, and the _____ of −0.3 is 0.3, because −0.3 + 0.3 = 0.
a. Thing
b. Additive inverse0
c. Undefined
d. Undefined

28. A _____ is a negotiable instrument instructing a financial institution to pay a specific amount of a specific currency from a specific demand account held in the maker/depositor's name with that institution. Both the maker and payee may be natural persons or legal entities.

a. Thing
c. Undefined
b. Check0
d. Undefined

29. The _____ is a property of multiplication or addition where the product or sum remains the same, regardless of whether or not the order of the addends or factors are changed.
   a. Thing
   b. Commutative property0
   c. Undefined
   d. Undefined

30. In geometry, a _____ is defined as a quadrilateral where all four of its angles are right angles.
   a. Thing
   b. Rectangle0
   c. Undefined
   d. Undefined

31. In plane geometry, a _____ is a polygon with four equal sides, four right angles, and parallel opposite sides. In algebra, the _____ of a number is that number multiplied by itself.
   a. Square0
   b. Thing
   c. Undefined
   d. Undefined

32. In mathematics the _____ refers to the identity: $a^2 - b^2 = (a+b)(a-b)$
   a. Thing
   b. Difference of two squares0
   c. Undefined
   d. Undefined

33. The term _____ can refer to an integer which is the square of some other integer, or an algebraic expression that can be factored as the square of some other expression.
   a. Perfect square0
   b. Thing
   c. Undefined
   d. Undefined

34. In mathematics, a _____ of a number x is a number r such that $r^2 = x$, or in words, a number r whose square (the result of multiplying the number by itself) is x.
   a. Thing
   b. Square root0
   c. Undefined
   d. Undefined

35. In mathematics, a _____ of a complex-valued function f is a member x of the domain of f such that f(x) vanishes at x, that is, $x : f(x) = 0$.
   a. Root0
   b. Thing
   c. Undefined
   d. Undefined

36. A _____ of a number is the product of that number with any integer.
   a. Thing
   b. Multiple0
   c. Undefined
   d. Undefined

37. A _____ is a three-dimensional solid object bounded by six square faces, facets, or sides, with three meeting at each vertex.
   a. Cube0
   b. Thing
   c. Undefined
   d. Undefined

38. _____ are of a number n in its third power-the result of multiplying it by itself three times.

Chapter 8. Factoring

   a. Cubes0
   c. Undefined
   b. Thing
   d. Undefined

39. _____ is a mathematical operation, written a^n, involving two numbers, the base a and the exponent n.
 - a. Thing
 - b. Exponentiating0
 - c. Undefined
 - d. Undefined

40. _____ is a mathematical operation, written a^n, involving two numbers, the base a and the exponent n.
 - a. Thing
 - b. Exponentiation0
 - c. Undefined
 - d. Undefined

41. A _____ is a number which is the cube of an integer.
 - a. Perfect cube0
 - b. Thing
 - c. Undefined
 - d. Undefined

42. A _____ signifies a point or points of probability on a subject e.g., the _____ of creativity, which allows for the formation of rule or norm or law by interpretation of the phenomena events that can be created.
 - a. Principle0
 - b. Thing
 - c. Undefined
 - d. Undefined

43. In Euclidean geometry, an _____ is a closed segment of a differentiable curve in the two-dimensional plane; for example, a circular _____ is a segment of a circle.
 - a. Arc0
 - b. Concept
 - c. Undefined
 - d. Undefined

44. In mathematics, a _____ is a polynomial equation of the second degree. The general form is $ax^2 + bx + c = 0$.
 - a. Thing
 - b. Quadratic equation0
 - c. Undefined
 - d. Undefined

45. In mathematics, _____ are essentially word problems that are designed to use mathematical critical thinking in everyday situations.
 - a. Application problems0
 - b. Thing
 - c. Undefined
 - d. Undefined

46. _____ means in succession or back-to-back
 - a. Thing
 - b. Consecutive0
 - c. Undefined
 - d. Undefined

47. _____ is a notation for writing numbers that is often used by scientists and mathematicians to make it easier to write large and small numbers.
 - a. Thing
 - b. Scientific notation0
 - c. Undefined
 - d. Undefined

48. _____ of an object is its speed in a particular direction.

Chapter 8. Factoring

a. Velocity0
b. Thing
c. Undefined
d. Undefined

49. Initial objects are also called _____, and terminal objects are also called final.
    a. Coterminal0
    b. Thing
    c. Undefined
    d. Undefined

50. A _____ is a number that is less than zero.
    a. Thing
    b. Negative number0
    c. Undefined
    d. Undefined

51. A _____ is one of the basic shapes of geometry: a polygon with three vertices and three sides which are straight line segments.
    a. Thing
    b. Triangle0
    c. Undefined
    d. Undefined

52. In Euclidean geometry, a _____ is the set of all points in a plane at a fixed distance, called the radius, from a given point, the center.
    a. Thing
    b. Circle0
    c. Undefined
    d. Undefined

53. In classical geometry, a _____ of a circle or sphere is any line segment from its center to its boundary. By extension, the _____ of a circle or sphere is the length of any such segment. The _____ is half the diameter. In science and engineering the term _____ of curvature is commonly used as a synonym for _____.
    a. Thing
    b. Radius0
    c. Undefined
    d. Undefined

54. In botany, _____ are above-ground plant organs specialized for photosynthesis. Their characteristics are typically analyzed by using Fiobonacci's sequences.
    a. Thing
    b. Leaves0
    c. Undefined
    d. Undefined

55. A _____ is a function that assigns a number to subsets of a given set.
    a. Measure0
    b. Thing
    c. Undefined
    d. Undefined

56. Regrouping is the act of putting ones into groups of 10. For example, the 1 on the far right of 131 would be denoted _____ if the digit of the number being subtracted is larger than 1, such as 131-99.
    a. Thing
    b. By 100
    c. Undefined
    d. Undefined

57. _____, Greek for "knowledge of nature," is the branch of science concerned with the discovery and characterization of universal laws which govern matter, energy, space, and time.
    a. Thing
    b. Physics0
    c. Undefined
    d. Undefined

Chapter 8. Factoring

58. In geometry, an _____ of a triangle is a straight line through a vertex and perpendicular to (i.e. forming a right angle with) the opposite side or an extension of the opposite side.
    a. Altitude0
    b. Concept
    c. Undefined
    d. Undefined

59. In mathematics, a _____ is a two-dimensional manifold or surface that is perfectly flat.
    a. Plane0
    b. Thing
    c. Undefined
    d. Undefined

60. In mathematics, a _____ can mean either an element of the set {1, 2, 3, ...} (i.e the positive integers or the counting numbers) or an element of the set {0, 1, 2, 3, ...} (i.e. the non-negative integers).
    a. Natural number0
    b. Thing
    c. Undefined
    d. Undefined

61. _____ are activities that are governed by a set of rules or customs and often engaged in competitively.
    a. Sports0
    b. Thing
    c. Undefined
    d. Undefined

62. _____ is a kind of property which exists as magnitude or multitude. It is among the basic classes of things along with quality, substance, change, and relation.
    a. Amount0
    b. Thing
    c. Undefined
    d. Undefined

63. The _____ of a solid object is the three-dimensional concept of how much space it occupies, often quantified numerically.
    a. Volume0
    b. Thing
    c. Undefined
    d. Undefined

64. In combinatorial mathematics, a _____ is an un-ordered collection of unique elements.
    a. Combination0
    b. Concept
    c. Undefined
    d. Undefined

65. _____ also sometimes known as the double distributive property or more colloquially as foiling, is commonly taught to US high school students learning algebra as a mnemonic for remembering how to multiply two binomials polynomials with two terms.
    a. FOIL method0
    b. Thing
    c. Undefined
    d. Undefined

66. The _____ is commonly taught to US high school students learning algebra as a mnemonic for remembering how to multiply two binomials.
    a. FOIL rule0
    b. Thing
    c. Undefined
    d. Undefined

67. In the scientific method, an _____ (Latin: ex-+-periri, "of (or from) trying"), is a set of actions and observations, performed in the context of solving a particular problem or question, in order to support or falsify a hypothesis or research concerning phenomena.

Chapter 8. Factoring

a. Experiment0
b. Thing
c. Undefined
d. Undefined

68. Acid _____ ratio measures the ability of a company to use its near cash or quick assets to immediately extinguish its current liabilities.
   a. Test0
   b. Thing
   c. Undefined
   d. Undefined

69. In a mathematical proof or a syllogism, a _____ is a statement that is the logical consequence of preceding statements.
   a. Conclusion0
   b. Concept
   c. Undefined
   d. Undefined

70. _____ means "constancy", i.e. if something retains a certain feature even after we change a way of looking at it, then it is symmetric.
   a. Symmetry0
   b. Thing
   c. Undefined
   d. Undefined

71. An _____ is when two lines intersect somewhere on a plane creating a right angle at intersection
   a. Thing
   b. Axes0
   c. Undefined
   d. Undefined

72. The _____ of measurement are a globally standardized and modernized form of the metric system.
   a. Thing
   b. Units0
   c. Undefined
   d. Undefined

73. _____ is the distance around a given two-dimensional object. As a general rule, the _____ of a polygon can always be calculated by adding all the length of the sides together. So, the formula for triangles is P = a + b + c, where a, b and c stand for each side of it. For quadrilaterals the equation is P = a + b + c + d. For equilateral polygons, P = na, where n is the number of sides and a is the side length.
   a. Thing
   b. Perimeter0
   c. Undefined
   d. Undefined

74. In mathematics, the conjugate _____ or adjoint matrix of an m-by-n matrix A with complex entries is the n-by-m matrix A* obtained from A by taking the transpose and then taking the complex conjugate of each entry.
   a. Thing
   b. Pairs0
   c. Undefined
   d. Undefined

75. _____ is a natural number that has exactly two distinct natural number divisors, which are 1 and the _____ itself.
   a. Prime number0
   b. Thing
   c. Undefined
   d. Undefined

76. In mathematics, an inequality is a statement about the relative size or order of two objects. For example 14 > 10, or 14 is _____ 10.

Chapter 8. Factoring

a. Greater than0
b. Thing
c. Undefined
d. Undefined

77. In mathematics, a _____ number (or a _____) is a natural number that has exactly two (distinct) natural number divisors, which are 1 and the _____ number itself.
    a. Prime0
    b. Thing
    c. Undefined
    d. Undefined

78. _____ (Greek Ἐﾓάθïóèὗíçò; 276 BC - 194 BC) was a Greek mathematician, geographer and astronomer.
    a. Eratosthenes0
    b. Person
    c. Undefined
    d. Undefined

79. A _____ number is a positive integer which has a positive divisor other than one or itself.
    a. Composite0
    b. Thing
    c. Undefined
    d. Undefined

80. _____ is a positive integer which has a positive divisor other than one or itself.
    a. Composite numbers0
    b. Thing
    c. Undefined
    d. Undefined

81. Marin _____, Marin Mersennus or le Père _____ was a French theologian, philosopher, mathematician and music theorist.
    a. Person
    b. Mersenne0
    c. Undefined
    d. Undefined

82. Mathematical _____ is used to represent ideas.
    a. Notation0
    b. Thing
    c. Undefined
    d. Undefined

83. An _____ or member of a set is an object that when collected together make up the set.
    a. Thing
    b. Element0
    c. Undefined
    d. Undefined

84. An _____ is an equality that remains true regardless of the values of any variables that appear within it, to distinguish it from an equality which is true under more particular conditions.
    a. Identity0
    b. Thing
    c. Undefined
    d. Undefined

85. In mathematics, an _____ (or neutral element) is a special type of element of a set with respect to a binary operation on that set.
    a. Concept
    b. Identity element0
    c. Undefined
    d. Undefined

86. In mathematics, the _____ inverse, or opposite, of a number n is the number that, when added to n, yields zero. The _____ inverse of n is denoted −n.

Chapter 8. Factoring

a. Additive0
b. Thing
c. Undefined
d. Undefined

87. In mathematics the _____ of a set which is equipped with the operation of addition is an element which, when added to any other element x in the set, yields x.
   a. Additive identity0
   b. Concept
   c. Undefined
   d. Undefined

88. _____, in economics and political economy, are the distributions or payments awarded to the various suppliers of the factors of production.
   a. Returns0
   b. Thing
   c. Undefined
   d. Undefined

89. In mathematics, the _____ of a function is the set of all "output" values produced by that function. Given a function $f : A \to B$, the _____ of f, is defined to be the set $\{x \in B : x = f(a)$ for some $a \in A\}$.
   a. Range0
   b. Thing
   c. Undefined
   d. Undefined

90. In mathematics, a _____ of a k-place relation $L \subseteq X_1 \times \ldots \times X_k$ is one of the sets X_j, $1 \leq j \leq k$. In the special case where k = 2 and $L \subseteq X_1 \times X_2$ is a function $L : X_1 \to X_2$, it is conventional to refer to X_1 as the _____ of the function and to refer to X_2 as the codomain of the function.
   a. Domain0
   b. Thing
   c. Undefined
   d. Undefined

91. A _____ is a unit of length, usually used to measure distance, in a number of different systems, including Imperial units, United States customary units and Norwegian/Swedish mil. Its size can vary from system to system, but in each is between 1 and 10 kilometers. In contemporary English contexts _____ refers to either:
   a. Thing
   b. Mile0
   c. Undefined
   d. Undefined

92. A _____ is a special kind of ratio, indicating a relationship between two measurements with different units, such as miles to gallons or cents to pounds.
   a. Thing
   b. Rate0
   c. Undefined
   d. Undefined

93. In finance and economics, _____ is the process of finding the present value of an amount of cash at some future date, and along with compounding cash forms the basis of time value of money calculations.
   a. Discount0
   b. Thing
   c. Undefined
   d. Undefined

94. The _____ is different from a more normal interest rate.
   a. Discount rate0
   b. Thing
   c. Undefined
   d. Undefined

95. _____ is the transport of people on a trip/journey or the process or time involved in a person or object moving from one location to another.

Chapter 8. Factoring

a. Thing
b. Travel0
c. Undefined
d. Undefined

96. _____ is electromagnetic radiation with a wavelength that is visible to the eye (visible _____) or, in a technical or scientific context, electromagnetic radiation of any wavelength.
a. Thing
b. Light0
c. Undefined
d. Undefined

97. _____ is the production of food, feed, fiber, fuel and other goods by the systematic raizing of plants and animals.
a. Thing
b. Agriculture0
c. Undefined
d. Undefined

98. Compass and straightedge or ruler-and-compass _____ is the _____ of lengths or angles using only an idealized ruler and compass.
a. Construction0
b. Thing
c. Undefined
d. Undefined

99. A _____ is a type of debt. All material things can be lent but this article focuses exclusively on monetary loans. Like all debt instruments, a _____ entails the redistribution of financial assets over time, between the lender and the borrower.
a. Loan0
b. Thing
c. Undefined
d. Undefined

100. _____ or investing is a term with several closely-related meanings in business management, finance and economics, related to saving or deferring consumption.
a. Investment0
b. Thing
c. Undefined
d. Undefined

101. The _____ is a popular form of gambling which involves the drawing of lots for a prize. Some governments forbid it, while others endorse it to the extent of organizign a national _____
a. Lottery0
b. Thing
c. Undefined
d. Undefined

102. In chemistry, a _____ is substance made by combining two or more different materials in such a way that no chemical reaction occurs.
a. Thing
b. Mixture0
c. Undefined
d. Undefined

103. _____ is a way of expressing a number as a fraction of 100 per cent meaning "per hundred".
a. Thing
b. Percent0
c. Undefined
d. Undefined

104. _____ is the process of recording pictures by means of capturing light on a light-sensitive medium, such as a film or sensor.

a. Photography0
c. Undefined
b. Thing
d. Undefined

105. _____ are a measure of time.
a. Minutes0
c. Undefined
b. Thing
d. Undefined

Chapter 9. Rational Expressions

1. A _____ is a numeral used to indicate a count. The most common use of the word today is to name the part of a fraction that tells the number or count of equal parts.
   a. Thing
   b. Numerator0
   c. Undefined
   d. Undefined

2. In mathematics, a _____ number is a number which can be expressed as a ratio of two integers. Non-integer _____ numbers (commonly called fractions) are usually written as the vulgar fraction a / b, where b is not zero.
   a. Thing
   b. Rational0
   c. Undefined
   d. Undefined

3. An _____ is a combination of numbers, operators, grouping symbols and/or free variables and bound variables arranged in a meaningful way which can be evaluated..
   a. Thing
   b. Expression0
   c. Undefined
   d. Undefined

4. In mathematics, a _____ is an expression that is constructed from one or more variables and constants, using only the operations of addition, subtraction, multiplication, and constant positive whole number exponents. is a _____. Note in particular that division by an expression containing a variable is not in general allowed in polynomials. [1]
   a. Polynomial0
   b. Thing
   c. Undefined
   d. Undefined

5. A _____ is the part of a fraction that tells how many equal parts make up a whole, and which is used in the name of the fraction: "halves", "thirds", "fourths" or "quarters", "fifths" and so on.
   a. Concept
   b. Denominator0
   c. Undefined
   d. Undefined

6. A _____ is a symbolic representation denoting a quantity or expression. It often represents an "unknown" quantity that has the potential to change.
   a. Variable0
   b. Thing
   c. Undefined
   d. Undefined

7. In mathematics, _____ is an elementary arithmetic operation. When one of the numbers is a whole number, _____ is the repeated sum of the other number.
   a. Thing
   b. Multiplication0
   c. Undefined
   d. Undefined

8. In mathematics, a _____ may be described informally as a number that can be given by an infinite decimal representation.
   a. Real number0
   b. Thing
   c. Undefined
   d. Undefined

9. _____ is the largest positive integer that divides both numbers without remainder.
   a. Thing
   b. Common Factor0
   c. Undefined
   d. Undefined

Chapter 9. Rational Expressions

10. In mathematics, factorization (British English: factorisation) or factoring is the decomposition of an object (for example, a number, a polynomial, or a matrix) into a product of other objects, or _____, which when multiplied together give the original.
    a. Thing
    b. Factors0
    c. Undefined
    d. Undefined

11. _____ is a mathematical operation, written a^n, involving two numbers, the base a and the exponent n.
    a. Thing
    b. Exponentiating0
    c. Undefined
    d. Undefined

12. _____ is a mathematical operation, written a^n, involving two numbers, the base a and the exponent n.
    a. Exponentiation0
    b. Thing
    c. Undefined
    d. Undefined

13. In mathematics, a _____ is the result of multiplying, or an expression that identifies factors to be multiplied.
    a. Thing
    b. Product0
    c. Undefined
    d. Undefined

14. In mathematics, the multiplicative inverse of a number x, denoted 1/x or x^{-1}, is the number which, when multiplied by x, yields 1. The multiplicative inverse of x is also called the _____ of x.
    a. Reciprocal0
    b. Thing
    c. Undefined
    d. Undefined

15. In common philosophical language, a proposition or _____, is the content of an assertion, that is, it is true-or-false and defined by the meaning of a particular piece of language.
    a. Concept
    b. Statement0
    c. Undefined
    d. Undefined

16. _____ or arithmetics is the oldest and most elementary branch of mathematics, used by almost everyone, for tasks ranging from simple daily counting to advanced science and business calculations.
    a. Thing
    b. Arithmetic0
    c. Undefined
    d. Undefined

17. A _____ of a number is the product of that number with any integer.
    a. Multiple0
    b. Thing
    c. Undefined
    d. Undefined

18. In mathematics, a _____ number (or a _____) is a natural number that has exactly two (distinct) natural number divisors, which are 1 and the _____ number itself.
    a. Prime0
    b. Thing
    c. Undefined
    d. Undefined

19. The _____ of two integers is the smallest positive integer that is a multiple of both intergers.
    a. Least common multiple0
    b. Thing
    c. Undefined
    d. Undefined

Chapter 9. Rational Expressions

20. In mathematics, _____ is the decomposition of an object into a product of other objects, or factors, which when multiplied together give the original.
    a. Factoring0
    b. Thing
    c. Undefined
    d. Undefined

21. _____, in number theory is the process of breaking down a composite number into smaller non-trivial divisors, which when multiplied together equal the original integer.
    a. Integer factorization0
    b. Thing
    c. Undefined
    d. Undefined

22. The _____ of a positive integer are the prime numbers that divide into that integer exactly, without leaving a remainder. The process of finding these numbers is called integer factorization, or prime factorization.
    a. Prime factor0
    b. Thing
    c. Undefined
    d. Undefined

23. In mathematics, a _____ is a constant multiplicative factor of a certain object. The object can be such things as a variable, a vector, a function, etc. For example, the _____ of $9x^2$ is 9.
    a. Thing
    b. Coefficient0
    c. Undefined
    d. Undefined

24. A _____ is the result of the addition of a set of numbers. The numbers may be natural numbers, complex numbers, matrices, or still more complicated objects. An infinite _____ is a subtle procedure known as a series.
    a. Sum0
    b. Thing
    c. Undefined
    d. Undefined

25. In mathematics, _____ are essentially word problems that are designed to use mathematical critical thinking in everyday situations.
    a. Application problems0
    b. Thing
    c. Undefined
    d. Undefined

26. _____ is the fee paid on borrowed money.
    a. Interest0
    b. Thing
    c. Undefined
    d. Undefined

27. In mathematics, _____ expressions is used to reduce the expression into the lowest possible term.
    a. Simplifying0
    b. Thing
    c. Undefined
    d. Undefined

28. A _____ is a negotiable instrument instructing a financial institution to pay a specific amount of a specific currency from a specific demand account held in the maker/depositor's name with that institution. Both the maker and payee may be natural persons or legal entities.
    a. Thing
    b. Check0
    c. Undefined
    d. Undefined

29. In mathematics, a _____ is the end result of a division problem. It can also be expressed as the number of times the divisor divides into the dividend.

Chapter 9. Rational Expressions

a. Quotient0
b. Thing
c. Undefined
d. Undefined

30. A _____ is a quantity that denotes the proportional amount or magnitude of one quantity relative to another.
   a. Thing
   b. Ratio0
   c. Undefined
   d. Undefined

31. The _____ of measurement are a globally standardized and modernized form of the metric system.
   a. Thing
   b. Units0
   c. Undefined
   d. Undefined

32. A _____ is a special kind of ratio, indicating a relationship between two measurements with different units, such as miles to gallons or cents to pounds.
   a. Rate0
   b. Thing
   c. Undefined
   d. Undefined

33. _____ is a special mathematical relationship between two quantities. Two quantities are called proportional if they vary in such a way that one of the quantities is a constant multiple of the other, or equivalently if they have a constant ratio.
   a. Thing
   b. Proportionality0
   c. Undefined
   d. Undefined

34. Two mathematical objects are equal if and only if they are precisely the same in every way. This defines a binary relation, _____, denoted by the sign of _____ "=" in such a way that the statement "x = y" means that x and y are equal.
   a. Equality0
   b. Thing
   c. Undefined
   d. Undefined

35. A _____ is a type of debt. All material things can be lent but this article focuses exclusively on monetary loans. Like all debt instruments, a _____ entails the redistribution of financial assets over time, between the lender and the borrower.
   a. Thing
   b. Loan0
   c. Undefined
   d. Undefined

36. _____ is a kind of property which exists as magnitude or multitude. It is among the basic classes of things along with quality, substance, change, and relation.
   a. Thing
   b. Amount0
   c. Undefined
   d. Undefined

37. A _____ is one of the basic shapes of geometry: a polygon with three vertices and three sides which are straight line segments.
   a. Thing
   b. Triangle0
   c. Undefined
   d. Undefined

38. _____ (or proportionality) are two quantities that vary in such a way that one of the quatities is a constant multiple of the other, or equivalently if they have a constant ratio.

Chapter 9. Rational Expressions

a. Thing
b. Proportions0
c. Undefined
d. Undefined

39. A pair of angles are said to be _____ if they share the same vertex and are bounded by the same pair of lines but are opposite to each other. They are also congruent.
a. Thing
b. Vertical angles0
c. Undefined
d. Undefined

40. In geometry and trigonometry, a _____ is defined as an angle between two straight intersecting lines of ninety degrees, or one-quarter of a circle.
a. Thing
b. Right angle0
c. Undefined
d. Undefined

41. _____ is a set, with some particular properties and usually some additional structure, such as the operations of addition or multiplication, for instance.
a. Space0
b. Thing
c. Undefined
d. Undefined

42. Compass and straightedge or ruler-and-compass _____ is the _____ of lengths or angles using only an idealized ruler and compass.
a. Thing
b. Construction0
c. Undefined
d. Undefined

43. In geometry, the _____ of a vertex of a polyhedron is the amount by which the sum of the angles of the faces at the vertex falls short of a full circle.
a. Thing
b. Defect0
c. Undefined
d. Undefined

44. _____ is a subset of a population.
a. Thing
b. Sample0
c. Undefined
d. Undefined

45. In navigation, a _____ is the clockwise angle between a reference direction and the direction to an object.
a. Bearing0
b. Thing
c. Undefined
d. Undefined

46. A bearing is a device to permit constrained relative motion between two parts, typically rotation or linear movement. _____ may be classified broadly according to the motions they allow and according to their principle of operation.
a. Thing
b. Bearings0
c. Undefined
d. Undefined

47. _____ (i.e. Plans) are a set of two-dimensional diagrams or _____ used to describe a place or object, or to communicate building or fabrication instructions.
a. Drawings0
b. Thing
c. Undefined
d. Undefined

Chapter 9. Rational Expressions

48. _____ is the estimation of a physical quantity such as distance, energy, temperature, or time.
   a. Measurement0
   b. Thing
   c. Undefined
   d. Undefined

49. A _____ is a vehicle, missile or aircraft which obtains thrust by the reaction to the ejection of fast moving fluid from within a _____ engine.
   a. Thing
   b. Rocket0
   c. Undefined
   d. Undefined

50. A _____ is a function that assigns a number to subsets of a given set.
   a. Measure0
   b. Thing
   c. Undefined
   d. Undefined

51. _____ is the production of food, feed, fiber, fuel and other goods by the systematic raizing of plants and animals.
   a. Agriculture0
   b. Thing
   c. Undefined
   d. Undefined

52. In mathematics, the _____ inverse of a number x, denoted $1/x$ or x^{-1}, is the number which, when multiplied by x, yields 1. The _____ inverse of x is also called the reciprocal of x.
   a. Multiplicative0
   b. Thing
   c. Undefined
   d. Undefined

53. The _____ are the only integral domain whose positive elements are well-ordered, and in which order is preserved by addition. Like the natural numbers, the _____ form a countably infinite set. The set of all _____ is usually denoted in mathematics by a boldface Z .
   a. Thing
   b. Integers0
   c. Undefined
   d. Undefined

54. _____ means in succession or back-to-back
   a. Thing
   b. Consecutive0
   c. Undefined
   d. Undefined

55. _____ element of an element x with respect to a binary operation * with identity element e is an element y such that $x * y = y * x = e$. In particular,
   a. Inverse0
   b. Thing
   c. Undefined
   d. Undefined

56. The _____ is a popular form of gambling which involves the drawing of lots for a prize. Some governments forbid it, while others endorse it to the extent of organizign a national _____
   a. Thing
   b. Lottery0
   c. Undefined
   d. Undefined

57. _____ are activities that are governed by a set of rules or customs and often engaged in competitively.
   a. Thing
   b. Sports0
   c. Undefined
   d. Undefined

Chapter 9. Rational Expressions

58. _____ is the process of recording pictures by means of capturing light on a light-sensitive medium, such as a film or sensor.
   a. Photography0
   b. Thing
   c. Undefined
   d. Undefined

59. The _____ is the distance around a closed curve. _____ is a kind of perimeter.
   a. Circumference0
   b. Thing
   c. Undefined
   d. Undefined

60. _____ is a synonym for information.
   a. Thing
   b. Data0
   c. Undefined
   d. Undefined

61. _____ (Greek Ἐñáõïóèÿíçò; 276 BC - 194 BC) was a Greek mathematician, geographer and astronomer.
   a. Eratosthenes0
   b. Person
   c. Undefined
   d. Undefined

62. A _____ is an information professional trained in library science and information science: the organization and management of information and service to people with information needs.
   a. Librarian0
   b. Thing
   c. Undefined
   d. Undefined

63. In Euclidean geometry, an _____ is a closed segment of a differentiable curve in the two-dimensional plane; for example, a circular _____ is a segment of a circle.
   a. Arc0
   b. Concept
   c. Undefined
   d. Undefined

64. _____ also called rectification of a curve—was historically difficult.
   a. Thing
   b. Arc length0
   c. Undefined
   d. Undefined

65. _____ primarily refers to social welfare service concerned with social protection, or protection against socially recognized conditions, including poverty, old age, disability, unemployment, families with children and others.
   a. Thing
   b. Social security0
   c. Undefined
   d. Undefined

66. _____, either of the curved-bracket punctuation marks that together make a set of _____
   a. Parentheses0
   b. Thing
   c. Undefined
   d. Undefined

67. In mathematics, and in particular in abstract algebra, the _____ is a property of binary operations that generalises the distributive law from elementary algebra.
   a. Distributive property0
   b. Thing
   c. Undefined
   d. Undefined

68. The word _____ comes from the Latin word linearis, which means created by lines.

a. Linear0
b. Thing
c. Undefined
d. Undefined

69. A _____ is an equation in which each term is either a constant or the product of a constant times the first power of a variable.
   a. Thing
   b. Linear equation0
   c. Undefined
   d. Undefined

70. _____ is a concept in traditional logic referring to a "type of immediate inference in which from a given proposition another proposition is inferred which has as its subject the predicate of the original proposition and as its predicate the subject of the original proposition (the quality of the proposition being retained)."
   a. Conversion0
   b. Concept
   c. Undefined
   d. Undefined

71. _____ is the design, analysis, and/or construction of works for practical purposes.
   a. Thing
   b. Engineering0
   c. Undefined
   d. Undefined

72. In classical geometry, a _____ of a circle or sphere is any line segment from its center to its boundary. By extension, the _____ of a circle or sphere is the length of any such segment. The _____ is half the diameter. In science and engineering the term _____ of curvature is commonly used as a synonym for _____.
   a. Radius0
   b. Thing
   c. Undefined
   d. Undefined

73. In mathematics, a _____ is a quadric surface, with the following equation in Cartesian coordinates: $(x/_a)^2 + (y/_b)^2 = 1$.
   a. Cylinder0
   b. Thing
   c. Undefined
   d. Undefined

74. _____, Greek for "knowledge of nature," is the branch of science concerned with the discovery and characterization of universal laws which govern matter, energy, space, and time.
   a. Physics0
   b. Thing
   c. Undefined
   d. Undefined

75. _____ is a physical property of a system that underlies the common notions of hot and cold; something that is hotter has the greater _____.
   a. Thing
   b. Temperature0
   c. Undefined
   d. Undefined

76. _____, from Latin meaning "to make progress", is defined in two different ways. Pure economic _____ is the increase in wealth that an investor has from making an investment, taking into consideration all costs associated with that investment including the opportunity cost of capital.
   a. Profit0
   b. Thing
   c. Undefined
   d. Undefined

Chapter 9. Rational Expressions

77. The _____ of a solid object is the three-dimensional concept of how much space it occupies, often quantified numerically.
   a. Thing
   b. Volume0
   c. Undefined
   d. Undefined

78. Fixed costs are expenses whose total does not change in proportion to the activity of a business.Unit fixed costs decline with volume following a retangular hyperbola as the volume of production.Variable costs by contrast change in relation to the activity of a business such as sales or production volume.Along with variable costs,fixed costs make up one of the two components of total cost. In the most simple production function total cost is equal to fixed costs plus variable costs.In accounting terminology, fixed costs will broadly include all costs which are not included in cost of goods sold, and variable costs are those captured in costs of goods sold. The implicit assumption required to make the equivalence between the accounting and economics terminology is that the accounting period is equal to the period in which fixed costs do not vary in relation to production. In practice, this equivalence does not always hold and depending on the period under consideration by management, some overhead expenses can be adjusted by management, and the specific allocation of each expense to each category will be decided under cost accounting.In business planning and management accounting, usage of the terms fixed costs, variable costs and others will often differ from usage in economics, and may depend on the intended use. For example, costs may be segregated into per unit costs fixed costs per period, and variable costs as a proportion of revenue. Capital expenditures will usually be allocated separately, and depending on the purpose, a portion may be regularly allocated to expenses as depreciation and amortization and seen as a _____ per period, or the entire amount may be considered upfront fixed costs.
   a. Fixed cost0
   b. Thing
   c. Undefined
   d. Undefined

79. _____ are expenses whose total does not change in proportion to the activity of a business, within the relevant time period or scale of production
   a. Thing
   b. Fixed costs0
   c. Undefined
   d. Undefined

80. _____ is a term used in marketing to indicate how much the price of a product is above the cost of producing and distributing the product.
   a. Thing
   b. Markup0
   c. Undefined
   d. Undefined

81. In mathematics, a matrix can be thought of as each row or _____ being a vector. Hence, a space formed by row vectors or _____ vectors are said to be a row space or a _____ space.
   a. Column0
   b. Concept
   c. Undefined
   d. Undefined

82. In a company, _____ is the sum of all financial records of salaries, wages, bonuses, and deductions.
   a. Thing
   b. Payroll0
   c. Undefined
   d. Undefined

83. _____ is the transport of people on a trip/journey or the process or time involved in a person or object moving from one location to another.

a. Travel0
b. Thing
c. Undefined
d. Undefined

84. In mathematics and the mathematical sciences, a _____ is a fixed, but possibly unspecified, value. This is in contrast to a variable, which is not fixed.
    a. Constant0
    b. Thing
    c. Undefined
    d. Undefined

85. In mathematics, a _____ is a two-dimensional manifold or surface that is perfectly flat.
    a. Plane0
    b. Thing
    c. Undefined
    d. Undefined

86. In mathematics and more specifically set theory, the _____ set is the unique set which contains no elements.
    a. Empty0
    b. Thing
    c. Undefined
    d. Undefined

87. Regrouping is the act of putting ones into groups of 10. For example, the 1 on the far right of 131 would be denoted _____ if the digit of the number being subtracted is larger than 1, such as 131-99.
    a. By 100
    b. Thing
    c. Undefined
    d. Undefined

88. In logic and mathematics, _____ is an operation on logical values, for example, the logical value of a proposition, that sends true to false and false to true.
    a. Negation0
    b. Person
    c. Undefined
    d. Undefined

89. In language and logic, quantification is a construct that specifies the quantity of individuals of the domain of discourse that apply to (or satisfy) an open formula. Language elements which generate quantifications are called _____.
    a. Thing
    b. Quantifiers0
    c. Undefined
    d. Undefined

90. In mathematics, a _____ or rhodonea curve is a sinusoid plotted in polar coordinates.
    a. Rose0
    b. Thing
    c. Undefined
    d. Undefined

91. _____ is a natural number that has exactly two distinct natural number divisors, which are 1 and the _____ itself.
    a. Prime number0
    b. Thing
    c. Undefined
    d. Undefined

92. In mathematics, an inequality is a statement about the relative size or order of two objects. For example 14 > 10, or 14 is _____ 10.
    a. Thing
    b. Greater than0
    c. Undefined
    d. Undefined

Chapter 9. Rational Expressions

93. _____ forms part of thinking. Considered the most complex of all intellectual functions, _____ has been defined as higher-order cognitive process that requires the modulation and control of more routine or fundamental skills.
   a. Thing
   b. Problem solving0
   c. Undefined
   d. Undefined

94. The act of _____ is the calculated approximation of a result which is usable even if input data may be incomplete, uncertain, or noisy.
   a. Estimating0
   b. Thing
   c. Undefined
   d. Undefined

95. _____ the expected value of a random variable displays the average or central value of the variable. It is a summary value of the distribution of the variable.
   a. Determining0
   b. Thing
   c. Undefined
   d. Undefined

96. In plane geometry, a _____ is a polygon with four equal sides, four right angles, and parallel opposite sides. In algebra, the _____ of a number is that number multiplied by itself.
   a. Thing
   b. Square0
   c. Undefined
   d. Undefined

97. In mathematics, a _____ is a mathematical statement which appears likely to be true, but has not been formally proven to be true under the rules of mathematical logic.
   a. Conjecture0
   b. Concept
   c. Undefined
   d. Undefined

98. In mathematics, a _____ can mean either an element of the set {1, 2, 3, ...} (i.e the positive integers or the counting numbers) or an element of the set {0, 1, 2, 3, ...} (i.e. the non-negative integers).
   a. Thing
   b. Natural number0
   c. Undefined
   d. Undefined

99. _____ are a measure of time.
   a. Minutes0
   b. Thing
   c. Undefined
   d. Undefined

100. A _____ is a method of using property as security for the payment of a debt.
   a. Mortgage0
   b. Thing
   c. Undefined
   d. Undefined

101. In economics _____ means before deductions brutto, e.g. _____ domestic or national product, or _____ profit or income
   a. Thing
   b. Gross0
   c. Undefined
   d. Undefined

102. _____, in law and economics, is a form of risk management primarily used to hedge against the risk of a contingent loss.

Chapter 9. Rational Expressions

a. Insurance0
c. Undefined
b. Thing
d. Undefined

103. The _____ or kilogramme is the SI base unit of mass. It is defined as being equal to the mass of the international prototype of the _____.
a. Kilogram0
c. Undefined
b. Thing
d. Undefined

104. _____ is electromagnetic radiation with a wavelength that is visible to the eye (visible _____) or, in a technical or scientific context, electromagnetic radiation of any wavelength.
a. Light0
c. Undefined
b. Thing
d. Undefined

105. _____ is the property of a physical object that quantifies the amount of matter and energy it is equivalent to.
a. Mass0
c. Undefined
b. Thing
d. Undefined

106. The metre (or _____, see spelling differences) is a measure of length. It is the basic unit of length in the metric system and in the International System of Units (SI), used around the world for general and scientific purposes.
a. Concept
c. Undefined
b. Meter0
d. Undefined

107. In mathematics a _____ is a function which defines a distance between elements of a set.
a. Metric0
c. Undefined
b. Thing
d. Undefined

108. The _____ is a decimalized system of measurement based on the metre and the gram.
a. Metric system0
c. Undefined
b. Concept
d. Undefined

109. In geometry, the _____ of an object is a point in some sense in the middle of the object.
a. Center0
c. Undefined
b. Thing
d. Undefined

110. In mathematics, a _____ is the set of all points in three-dimensional space (R^3) which are at distance r from a fixed point of that space, where r is a positive real number called the radius of the _____. The fixed point is called the center or centre, and is not part of the _____ itself.
a. Sphere0
c. Undefined
b. Thing
d. Undefined

111. In geometry and physics, _____ are half-lines that continue forever in one direction.
a. Thing
c. Undefined
b. Rays0
d. Undefined

112. In Euclidean geometry, a uniform _____ is a linear transformation that enlargers or diminishes objects, and whose _____ factor is the same in all directions. This is also called homothethy.

Chapter 9. Rational Expressions

a. Scale0
b. Thing
c. Undefined
d. Undefined

113. In geometry, a _____ (Greek words diairo = divide and metro = measure) of a circle is any straight line segment that passes through the centre and whose endpoints are on the circular boundary, or, in more modern usage, the length of such a line segment. When using the word in the more modern sense, one speaks of the _____ rather than a _____, because all diameters of a circle have the same length. This length is twice the radius. The _____ of a circle is also the longest chord that the circle has.

a. Thing
b. Diameter0
c. Undefined
d. Undefined

114. A _____, as defined by the International Astronomical Union, is a celestial body orbiting a star or stellar remnant that is massive enough to be rounded by its own gravity, not massive enough to cause thermonuclear fusion in its core, and has cleared its neighboring region of planetesimals.

a. Thing
b. Planet0
c. Undefined
d. Undefined

115. In mathematics, the additive inverse, or _____ of a number n is the number that, when added to n, yields zero. The additive inverse of n is denoted −n. For example, 7 is −7, because 7 + (−7) = 0, and the additive inverse of −0.3 is 0.3, because −0.3 + 0.3 = 0.

a. Thing
b. Opposite0
c. Undefined
d. Undefined

116. In mathematics, the _____ of a number n is the number that, when added to n, yields zero. The _____ of n is denoted −n. For example, 7 is −7, because 7 + (−7) = 0, and the _____ of −0.3 is 0.3, because −0.3 + 0.3 = 0.

a. Thing
b. Additive inverse0
c. Undefined
d. Undefined

117. _____ are procedures that allow people to exchange information by one of several methods.

a. Communications0
b. Thing
c. Undefined
d. Undefined

118. In mathematics, the concept of a _____ tries to capture the intuitive idea of a geometrical one-dimensional and continuous object. A simple example is the circle.

a. Curve0
b. Thing
c. Undefined
d. Undefined

119. In chemistry, a _____ is substance made by combining two or more different materials in such a way that no chemical reaction occurs.

a. Mixture0
b. Thing
c. Undefined
d. Undefined

Chapter 10. Radical Expressions

1. If one number is to the right of another number on the number line, this number is <U>greater than </U>the number on the left. The symbol that is used is >.
   - a. -equivalence
   - b. Greater than10
   - c. Undefined
   - d. Undefined

2. An _____ combines numbers, operators, and/or variables but contains no equal or inequality sign.
   - a. Expression10
   - b. ADE classification
   - c. Undefined
   - d. Undefined

3. _____ is used synonymously for variable.
   - a. Factor10
   - b. -equivalence
   - c. Undefined
   - d. Undefined

4. A _____ is the result of multiplying, or an expression that identifies factors to be multiplied
   - a. Product10
   - b. -equivalence
   - c. Undefined
   - d. Undefined

5. _____ are intuitively defined as numbers that are in one-to-one correspondence with the points on an infinite line—the number line. The term "real number" is a retronym coined in response to "imaginary number" _____ may be rational or irrational; algebraic or transcendental; and positive, negative, or zero _____ measure continuous quantities. They may in theory be expressed by decimal fractions that have an infinite sequence of digits to the right of the decimal point; these are often (mis-)represented in the same form as 324.823211247... (where the three dots express that there would still be more digits to come, no matter how many more might be added at the end).
   - a. -equivalence
   - b. Real numbers10
   - c. Undefined
   - d. Undefined

6. The very fact that we are measuring objects with respect to some characteristic implies that the objects differ in that characteristic; or stated in another way, that the characteristic can take on a number of different values. These properties or characteristics of an object that can assume two or more different values are referred to as a _____.
   - a. -equivalence
   - b. Variable10
   - c. Undefined
   - d. Undefined

7. The <U>exponent </U>indicates how many of the base to multiply together to get the product. When 5 to the third power is 125, then 3 is the _____ and can also be called a power.
   - a. Exponent10
   - b. ADE classification
   - c. Undefined
   - d. Undefined

8. _____ are characteristics or properties of an object that can take on one or more different values.
   - a. -equivalence
   - b. Variables10
   - c. Undefined
   - d. Undefined

9. Another word for independent variables in the analysis of variance is _____.
   - a. Factors10
   - b. -equivalence
   - c. Undefined
   - d. Undefined

Chapter 10. Radical Expressions

10. _____ (from the Greek words Geo = earth and metro = measure) is the branch of mathematics first popularized in ancient Greek culture by Thales (circa 624-547 BC) dealing with spatial relationships. The earliest beginnings of _____ may be traced to Ancient Egypt
   a. -equivalence
   b. Geometry10
   c. Undefined
   d. Undefined

11. _____ consist of 0,1,2,3,4,5,....
   a. Whole numbers10
   b. -equivalence
   c. Undefined
   d. Undefined

12. The answer to subtraction is called the <U>difference</U>.
   a. Difference10
   b. -equivalence
   c. Undefined
   d. Undefined

13. Addition (or summation) is one of the basic operations of arithmetic. In its simplest form, addition combines two numbers, the augend and addend, into a single number, the _____. Adding more numbers can be viewed as repeated addition. (Repeated addition of the number one is the most basic form of counting.) By extension, the addition of zero numbers, one number, or infinitely many numbers can be defined.
   a. Sum10
   b. -equivalence
   c. Undefined
   d. Undefined

14. A _____ is a number or variable, or the product or quotient of a number or variable.
   a. Term10
   b. -equivalence
   c. Undefined
   d. Undefined

15. _____ is the property of multiplication over addition which demonstrates that for all numbers a,b,c; a(b+c)=ab+ac, and ab+ac=a(b+c).
   a. -equivalence
   b. Distributive Property10
   c. Undefined
   d. Undefined

16. A _____ is the end result of a division problem. For example, in the problem 6 ÷ 3, the _____ would be 2, while 6 would be called the dividend, and 3 the divisor
   a. Quotient10
   b. -equivalence
   c. Undefined
   d. Undefined

17. The bottom part of any fraction represents the number of pieces in one whole unit. This bottom part is called the <U>denominator.</U>
   a. -equivalence
   b. Denominator10
   c. Undefined
   d. Undefined

18. The top part of the fraction is called the <U>numerator</U>. It could also be called the dividend, but _____ is preferred.
   a. Numerator10
   b. -equivalence
   c. Undefined
   d. Undefined

Chapter 10. Radical Expressions

19. <U>Multiplication</U> is a quick way of adding identical numbers. For example, the sum 7 + 7 + 7 can be found by multiplying 3 times 7. This model is reflected in the use of the word times as a synonym for multiplied by. The resuult of multiplying numbers is called a product. The numbers being multiplied are called factors.
   a. -equivalence
   b. Multiplication10
   c. Undefined
   d. Undefined

20. A _____ is the relationship between two quantities. It is expressed as the quotient of two numbers, or as two numbers separated by a colon (pronounced "to"). A number that can be written as a _____ of two integers is a rational number.
   a. Ratio10
   b. -equivalence
   c. Undefined
   d. Undefined

21. Whenever a number is raised to the second power, we can also say that the number is _____.
   a. -equivalence
   b. Squared10
   c. Undefined
   d. Undefined

22. By _____ we mean collecting observations made upon our environment -- observations, which are the results of measurements using clocks, balances, measuring rods, counting operations, or other objectively defined measuring instruments or procedures. _____ may mean simply counting the number of times a particular property occurs.
   a. -equivalence
   b. Data10
   c. Undefined
   d. Undefined

23. A _____ refers to the distance or difference between any score in a distribution of data from the mean.
   a. Deviation10
   b. -equivalence
   c. Undefined
   d. Undefined

24. The same statistical principles apply to the evaluation of observed _____ between sets of data. The field of statistics provides the necessary techniques for making statements of our certainty that there are real as opposed to chance _____.
   a. -equivalence
   b. Differences10
   c. Undefined
   d. Undefined

25. The most important measure of central tendency, and one of the basic building blocks of all statistical analysis, is the arithmetic _____. It is simply the sum of all the set of values divided by the number of values involved. As a measure of central tendency, it is affected by extreme scores, and it assumes a ratio scale of measurement.
   a. -equivalence
   b. Mean10
   c. Undefined
   d. Undefined

26. A _____ is a concrete example of an item or a specification against which all others may be measured. For example, there are "primary standards" for length, mass (see Kilogram standard), and other units of measure, kept by laboratories and standards organizations.
   a. -equivalence
   b. Standard10
   c. Undefined
   d. Undefined

27. A measure of variability in a distribution, the _____ is the square root of the variance. The _____ measures the variability of scores around the mean: the standardized difference. It is the square root of the mean square error.

Chapter 10. Radical Expressions

a. Standard deviation10
c. Undefined
b. -equivalence
d. Undefined

28. A _____ is a well-defined collection of objects considered as a whole.
a. Set10
c. Undefined
b. -equivalence
d. Undefined

29. The Greek letter _____ indicates summation.
a. -equivalence
c. Undefined
b. Sigma10
d. Undefined

30. Any polygon that has 3 sides is called a <U>triangle</U>.
a. -equivalence
c. Undefined
b. Triangle10
d. Undefined

31. A <U>hypotenuse </U>occurs in a right triangle and is the side opposite the right angle. It will also be the longest side of a right triangle.
a. -equivalence
c. Undefined
b. Hypotenuse10
d. Undefined

32. By _____ we mean the cumulative frequency, counting in from the nearer end.
a. -equivalence
c. Undefined
b. Depth10
d. Undefined

33. A number that is raised to a power, or _____ of an exponential function. This finds common use, for example, in the depiction of numbers, for instance, 10 is the _____ used in the decimal system, whereas 2 is the _____ in the binary numeral system.
a. -equivalence
c. Undefined
b. Base10
d. Undefined

34. A number that does not change in value in a given situation is a _____.
a. -equivalence
c. Undefined
b. Constant10
d. Undefined

Chapter 11. Quadratic Equations

1. A _____ is a class of simple functions where they are constructed using only multiplication and addition of terms.
   - a. -equivalence
   - b. Polynomial11
   - c. Undefined
   - d. Undefined

2. A _____ is a concrete example of an item or a specification against which all others may be measured. For example, there are "primary standards" for length, mass (see Kilogram standard), and other units of measure, kept by laboratories and standards organizations.
   - a. -equivalence
   - b. Standard11
   - c. Undefined
   - d. Undefined

3. factorization or _____ is the decomposition of an object (for example, a number, a polynomial, or a matrix) into a product of other objects, or factors, which when multiplied together give the original. For example, the number 15 factors into primes as 3 × 5; and the polynomial $x2 - 4$ factors as $(x - 2)(x + 2)$. In both cases, we obtain a product of simpler things.
   - a. Factoring11
   - b. -equivalence
   - c. Undefined
   - d. Undefined

4. An _____ combines numbers, operators, and/or variables but contains no equal or inequality sign.
   - a. ADE classification
   - b. Expression11
   - c. Undefined
   - d. Undefined

5. _____ is used synonymously for variable.
   - a. Factor11
   - b. -equivalence
   - c. Undefined
   - d. Undefined

6. A _____ is simply a polynomial with two terms such as this example: $2x + 7$.
   - a. Binomial11
   - b. -equivalence
   - c. Undefined
   - d. Undefined

7. A _____ is a multiplicative factor of a certain object such as a variable (for example, the coefficients of a polynomial), a basis vector, a basis function and so on. Usually, the objects and the coefficients are indexed in the same way, leading to expressions such as $a_1x_1 + a_2x_2 + a_3x_3 + ...$ where a_n is the _____ of the variable x_n for each $n = 1, 2, 3, ...$
   - a. Coefficient11
   - b. -equivalence
   - c. Undefined
   - d. Undefined

8. A number that does not change in value in a given situation is a _____.
   - a. Constant11
   - b. -equivalence
   - c. Undefined
   - d. Undefined

9. A _____ is a number or variable, or the product or quotient of a number or variable.
   - a. Term11
   - b. -equivalence
   - c. Undefined
   - d. Undefined

10. A _____ is simply a polynomial with three terms connect by addition and multiplication.
    - a. Trinomial11
    - b. -equivalence
    - c. Undefined
    - d. Undefined

Chapter 11. Quadratic Equations

11. A _____ is a number that when multiplied by a given number gives you one. This is also called multiplicative inverse.
    a. Reciprocal11
    b. -equivalence
    c. Undefined
    d. Undefined

12. The word _____ can have three meanings: In _____ theory, a _____ is an abstract object consisting of vertices (or nodes) and edges (or arcs) between pairs of vertices. The _____ of a function f : X ¨ Y is the set of all pairs (x,f(x)) The _____ of a relation, a generalisation of the _____ of a function.
    a. -equivalence
    b. Graph11
    c. Undefined
    d. Undefined

13. The _____ is t the point where a graph intersects the y-axis and is found by setting x = 0 and then sovling for the y-value.
    a. -equivalence
    b. Y-intercept11
    c. Undefined
    d. Undefined

14. _____ are characteristics or properties of an object that can take on one or more different values.
    a. Variables11
    b. -equivalence
    c. Undefined
    d. Undefined

15. _____ is implied when data values are distributed in the same way above and below the middle of the sample.
    a. Symmetry11
    b. -equivalence
    c. Undefined
    d. Undefined

16. A _____ is a mathematical function when plotted on an x,y graph forms a straight line.
    a. Linear function11
    b. -equivalence
    c. Undefined
    d. Undefined

17. The very fact that we are measuring objects with respect to some characteristic implies that the objects differ in that characteristic; or stated in another way, that the characteristic can take on a number of different values. These properties or characteristics of an object that can assume two or more different values are referred to as a _____.
    a. -equivalence
    b. Variable11
    c. Undefined
    d. Undefined

18. Addition (or summation) is one of the basic operations of arithmetic. In its simplest form, addition combines two numbers, the augend and addend, into a single number, the _____. Adding more numbers can be viewed as repeated addition. (Repeated addition of the number one is the most basic form of counting.) By extension, the addition of zero numbers, one number, or infinitely many numbers can be defined.
    a. -equivalence
    b. Sum11
    c. Undefined
    d. Undefined

19. _____ (from the Greek words Geo = earth and metro = measure) is the branch of mathematics first popularized in ancient Greek culture by Thales (circa 624-547 BC) dealing with spatial relationships. The earliest beginnings of _____ may be traced to Ancient Egypt

Chapter 11. Quadratic Equations

a. -equivalence
c. Undefined

b. Geometry11
d. Undefined

20. The answer to subtraction is called the <U>difference</U>.
   a. Difference11
   c. Undefined

   b. -equivalence
   d. Undefined

21. The _____ is the point where a graph intersects the x-axis and is found by letting y = 0 and then solving for the x-value.
   a. X-intercept11
   c. Undefined

   b. -equivalence
   d. Undefined

22. _____ is a convenient way to write very large and very small numbers. , for example, means one billion (a 1 followed by nine zeros: 1,000,000,000). means one billionth, or 0.000000001. Writing 109 instead of nine zeros saves the reader and the writer the effort and hazard of counting a long string of zeros to see how large the number is.
   a. Scientific notation11
   c. Undefined

   b. -equivalence
   d. Undefined

23. _____ is the study of quantity, structure, space, and change. Historically, _____ developed from counting, calculation, measurement, and the study of the shapes and motions of physical objects, through the use of abstraction and deductive reasoning.
   a. -equivalence
   c. Undefined

   b. Mathematics11
   d. Undefined

24. A number that is raised to a power, or _____ of an exponential function. This finds common use, for example, in the depiction of numbers, for instance, 10 is the _____ used in the decimal system, whereas 2 is the _____ in the binary numeral system.
   a. -equivalence
   c. Undefined

   b. Base11
   d. Undefined

25. Any polygon that has 3 sides is called a <U>triangle</U>.
   a. Triangle11
   c. Undefined

   b. -equivalence
   d. Undefined

26. _____ is an estimate of the decrease in the value of an asset, caused by "wear and tear", obsolescence, or impairment. The use of _____ affects a company's (or an individual's) financial statements, and, in some countries, their taxes.
   a. -equivalence
   c. Undefined

   b. Depreciation11
   d. Undefined

27. A <U>hypotenuse </U>occurs in a right triangle and is the side opposite the right angle. It will also be the longest side of a right triangle.
   a. -equivalence
   c. Undefined

   b. Hypotenuse11
   d. Undefined

ANSWER KEY

Chapter 1

1. b	2. a	3. a	4. b	5. b	6. a	7. b	8. b	9. b	10. a
11. b	12. a	13. b	14. a	15. a	16. b	17. a	18. b	19. a	20. b
21. b	22. a	23. a	24. a	25. a	26. b	27. b	28. a	29. b	30. b
31. a	32. b	33. b	34. b	35. b	36. a	37. a	38. a	39. b	40. b
41. b	42. b	43. a	44. a	45. a	46. b	47. b	48. a	49. a	50. a
51. a	52. a	53. b	54. a	55. a	56. b	57. a	58. a	59. b	60. b
61. b	62. a	63. a	64. a	65. a	66. a	67. a	68. b	69. b	70. a
71. a	72. b	73. b	74. b	75. b	76. b	77. b	78. a	79. b	80. a
81. b	82. a	83. a	84. b	85. a	86. b	87. a	88. a	89. b	90. a
91. b	92. a	93. b	94. a	95. a	96. a	97. a	98. a	99. b	100. a
101. b	102. a	103. b	104. a						

Chapter 2

1. a	2. a	3. a	4. a	5. a	6. a	7. a	8. a	9. b	10. b
11. a	12. a	13. a	14. a	15. b	16. b	17. b	18. b	19. a	20. b
21. a	22. a	23. b	24. a	25. a	26. b	27. a	28. a	29. b	30. a
31. b	32. b	33. a	34. b	35. b	36. b	37. a	38. a	39. a	40. a
41. b	42. a	43. a	44. a	45. b	46. b	47. a	48. a	49. a	50. a
51. b	52. b	53. a	54. a	55. a	56. b	57. a	58. b	59. b	60. b
61. b	62. a	63. b	64. a	65. b	66. a	67. a	68. b	69. b	70. a
71. a	72. a	73. a	74. a	75. a	76. b	77. a	78. a	79. a	80. a
81. a	82. b	83. a	84. b	85. b	86. b	87. a	88. b	89. a	90. a
91. b	92. b	93. a	94. b						

Chapter 3

1. b	2. a	3. b	4. b	5. a	6. b	7. b	8. a	9. a	10. a
11. a	12. b	13. b	14. b	15. b	16. a	17. a	18. a	19. b	20. b
21. a	22. a	23. b	24. a	25. b	26. a	27. a	28. b	29. a	30. b
31. a	32. a	33. b	34. b	35. a	36. b	37. b	38. b	39. b	40. b
41. b	42. b	43. b	44. a	45. a	46. a	47. b	48. a	49. a	50. a
51. a	52. b	53. b	54. a	55. a	56. a	57. a	58. b	59. a	60. b
61. b	62. a	63. b	64. a	65. b	66. a	67. b	68. a	69. a	70. a
71. b	72. b	73. a	74. a	75. a	76. b	77. a	78. b	79. b	80. b
81. b	82. b	83. b	84. a	85. b	86. b	87. b	88. b	89. b	90. b
91. a	92. b	93. b	94. a	95. b	96. a	97. a	98. a	99. a	100. b
101. b	102. b	103. b	104. b	105. a	106. a	107. a	108. a	109. a	110. a

Chapter 4

1. b	2. b	3. b	4. a	5. a	6. a	7. b	8. b	9. b	10. b
11. b	12. a	13. a	14. a	15. a	16. b	17. b	18. b	19. a	20. a
21. a	22. a	23. a	24. b	25. b	26. b	27. b	28. a	29. a	30. a
31. a	32. b	33. a	34. a	35. a	36. b	37. b	38. a	39. a	40. b
41. b	42. a	43. a	44. b	45. a	46. a	47. a	48. a	49. a	50. a
51. a	52. b	53. a	54. b	55. a	56. b	57. a	58. b	59. b	60. b
61. a	62. b	63. b	64. b	65. a	66. b	67. a	68. b	69. a	70. a
71. a	72. b	73. a	74. a	75. b	76. b	77. b	78. b	79. a	80. a
81. a	82. b	83. a	84. a	85. b	86. a	87. a	88. b	89. b	90. b
91. b	92. a	93. b	94. a	95. b	96. a	97. b	98. a	99. a	100. b
101. a	102. b	103. b	104. b	105. b	106. b	107. b	108. a	109. a	110. b
111. b	112. a	113. b	114. b	115. b	116. a	117. b	118. a	119. a	120. a
121. b	122. a	123. b	124. a	125. a	126. b	127. b	128. b	129. a	130. a
131. b	132. b	133. b	134. a	135. b	136. a	137. a	138. a	139. b	140. b
141. a	142. b	143. a	144. b	145. a	146. b	147. a	148. a		

Chapter 5

1. a	2. b	3. b	4. b	5. a	6. a	7. a	8. b	9. a	10. a
11. b	12. a	13. a	14. b	15. b	16. b	17. b	18. b	19. b	20. b
21. b	22. a	23. a	24. a	25. a	26. b	27. b	28. a	29. a	30. a
31. b	32. a	33. b	34. b	35. a	36. b	37. a	38. b	39. a	40. a
41. b	42. a	43. b	44. b	45. a	46. a	47. a	48. b	49. b	50. b
51. b	52. b	53. b	54. b	55. a	56. a	57. b	58. a	59. a	60. a
61. a	62. a	63. a	64. b	65. a	66. a	67. b	68. b	69. b	70. a
71. b	72. a	73. b	74. a	75. b	76. a	77. b	78. a	79. a	80. b
81. b	82. b	83. a	84. a	85. b	86. b	87. b	88. b	89. a	90. b
91. a	92. a	93. a	94. b	95. a	96. a	97. b	98. b	99. a	100. a
101. a	102. b	103. a	104. b	105. a	106. b	107. b	108. b	109. a	

Chapter 6

1. b	2. b	3. b	4. b	5. a	6. b	7. a	8. a	9. a	10. b
11. b	12. a	13. a	14. b	15. b	16. a	17. b	18. a	19. a	20. b
21. a	22. a	23. b	24. b	25. a	26. b	27. b	28. a	29. a	30. a
31. b	32. b	33. a	34. b	35. b	36. a	37. b	38. b	39. a	40. a
41. b	42. b	43. b	44. b	45. b	46. b	47. b	48. b	49. a	50. a
51. a	52. b	53. b	54. a	55. a	56. a	57. b	58. b	59. a	60. a
61. b	62. a	63. a	64. b	65. b	66. a	67. a	68. a	69. b	70. b
71. b	72. b	73. a	74. a	75. b	76. a	77. a	78. b	79. b	80. b
81. a	82. a	83. b	84. b						

ANSWER KEY

Chapter 7

1. b	2. a	3. b	4. b	5. b	6. b	7. a	8. b	9. a	10. a
11. b	12. a	13. a	14. b	15. b	16. b	17. a	18. b	19. a	20. a
21. b	22. b	23. a	24. a	25. a	26. b	27. a	28. a	29. b	30. b
31. a	32. b	33. a	34. b	35. b	36. b	37. b	38. b	39. a	40. b
41. a	42. b	43. a	44. b	45. a	46. b	47. a	48. a	49. a	50. a
51. a	52. b	53. b	54. a	55. a	56. b	57. b	58. a	59. a	60. b
61. a	62. b	63. b	64. a	65. a	66. a	67. a	68. b	69. b	70. a
71. a	72. b	73. a	74. b	75. b	76. b	77. a	78. a	79. a	80. a
81. b	82. b	83. b	84. a	85. b	86. a	87. b	88. b	89. b	90. a
91. b	92. a	93. b	94. a	95. a	96. a	97. a	98. a	99. a	100. b
101. a	102. b	103. b							

Chapter 8

1. b	2. b	3. b	4. b	5. a	6. b	7. a	8. a	9. b	10. a
11. a	12. a	13. a	14. a	15. a	16. a	17. a	18. a	19. a	20. a
21. a	22. a	23. a	24. b	25. a	26. b	27. b	28. b	29. b	30. b
31. a	32. b	33. a	34. b	35. a	36. b	37. a	38. a	39. b	40. b
41. a	42. a	43. a	44. b	45. a	46. b	47. b	48. a	49. a	50. b
51. b	52. b	53. b	54. b	55. a	56. b	57. b	58. a	59. a	60. a
61. a	62. a	63. a	64. a	65. a	66. a	67. a	68. a	69. a	70. a
71. b	72. b	73. b	74. b	75. a	76. a	77. a	78. a	79. a	80. a
81. b	82. a	83. b	84. a	85. b	86. a	87. a	88. a	89. a	90. a
91. b	92. a	93. a	94. a	95. b	96. b	97. b	98. a	99. a	100. a
101. a	102. b	103. b	104. a	105. a					

Chapter 9

1. b	2. b	3. b	4. a	5. b	6. a	7. b	8. a	9. b	10. b
11. b	12. a	13. b	14. a	15. b	16. b	17. a	18. a	19. a	20. a
21. a	22. a	23. b	24. a	25. a	26. a	27. a	28. b	29. a	30. b
31. b	32. a	33. b	34. a	35. b	36. b	37. b	38. b	39. b	40. b
41. a	42. b	43. b	44. b	45. a	46. b	47. a	48. a	49. b	50. a
51. a	52. a	53. b	54. b	55. a	56. b	57. b	58. a	59. a	60. b
61. a	62. a	63. a	64. b	65. b	66. a	67. a	68. a	69. b	70. a
71. b	72. a	73. a	74. a	75. b	76. a	77. b	78. a	79. b	80. b
81. a	82. b	83. a	84. a	85. a	86. a	87. a	88. a	89. b	90. a
91. a	92. b	93. b	94. a	95. a	96. b	97. a	98. b	99. a	100. a
101. b	102. a	103. a	104. a	105. a	106. b	107. a	108. a	109. a	110. a
111. b	112. a	113. b	114. b	115. b	116. b	117. a	118. a	119. a	

Chapter 10

1. b	2. a	3. a	4. a	5. b	6. b	7. a	8. b	9. a	10. b
11. a	12. a	13. a	14. a	15. b	16. a	17. b	18. a	19. b	20. a
21. b	22. b	23. a	24. b	25. b	26. b	27. a	28. a	29. b	30. b
31. b	32. b	33. b	34. b						

Chapter 11

1. b	2. b	3. a	4. b	5. a	6. a	7. a	8. a	9. a	10. a
11. a	12. b	13. b	14. a	15. a	16. a	17. b	18. b	19. b	20. a
21. a	22. a	23. b	24. b	25. a	26. b	27. b			

www.ingramcontent.com/pod-product-compliance
Lightning Source LLC
Chambersburg PA
CBHW082048230426
43670CB00016B/2820